WEATHERED

Finding Strength
on the John Muir Trail

Christy Teglo

Weathered: Finding Strength on the John Muir Trail

ISBN: 978-1-7375900-0-2 (print)

Editor: Sandra Childress

Cover design, publishing logo, and map illustration created by Ian Bright (www.BrightRoseBooks.com)

Interior design: Susan Gerber

*Dedicated to the friends and family
who believed in me, even when I didn't*

Contents

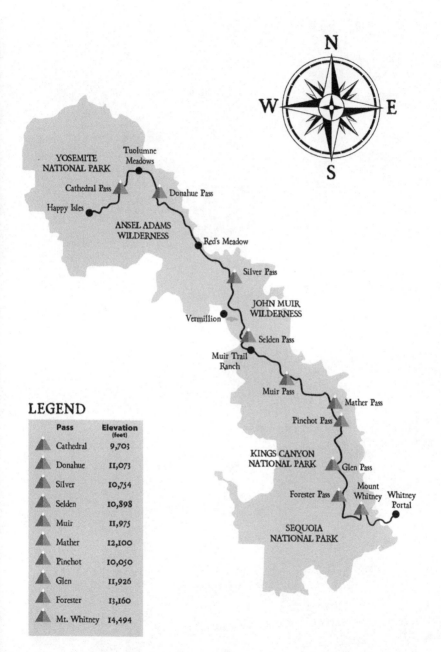

LEGEND

Pass	Elevation (feet)
Cathedral	9,703
Donahue	11,073
Silver	10,754
Selden	10,898
Muir	11,975
Mather	12,100
Pinchot	10,050
Glen	11,926
Forester	13,160
Mt. Whitney	14,494

YOSEMITE
NATIONAL PARK

Tuolumne
Meadows

Cathedral Pass

Happy Isles

Donahue Pass

ANSEL ADAMS
WILDERNESS

Red's Meadow

Silver Pass

JOHN MUIR
WILDERNESS

Vermillion

Selden Pass

Muir Trail
Ranch

Muir Pass

Mather Pass

Pinchot Pass

KINGS CANYON
NATIONAL PARK

Glen Pass

Mount
Whitney

Whitney
Portal

Forester Pass

SEQUOIA
NATIONAL PARK

N

W   E

S

What is the JMT?

It was February 2016 when a coworker, Barry, told me about the John Muir Trail, or JMT. We were talking about vacations that we wanted to take that year. He said the JMT was a trail that covered more than 200 miles in the California High Sierra mountains that started in Yosemite Valley and finished at Mount Whitney.

I had not heard of Mount Whitney. I asked, "Mount Whitney? Tell me more about the trail." Barry explained, "Mount Whitney is the tallest mountain in the contiguous United States. The JMT is 211 miles (plus another 11 miles coming down from Whitney). The whole trail is at high elevation, and Whitney is at 14,500 feet. The trail goes over ten mountain passes. It's a *no-joke* trail."

Barry showed me pictures of the trail online, and it looked amazing. He also explained that he tried to hike 200 miles on the east coast with a friend after graduating from college a couple of years ago and only made it 100 miles. They had to bail because it rained so much and his friend was miserable.

I went back to my desk and thought, *that sounds fun, challenging, and beautiful.* Within a week, I was looking at the trail online, and the pictures were breathtaking. With the exception of the first seven miles, the trail doesn't drop below 7,000 feet and much of the trail is over 10,000 feet. The total amount of elevation gain is 47,000 feet and the total amount of descent is 38,000 feet. For comparison, Mount Everest is 29,029 feet from sea level to the peak.

I researched the permit process on the Yosemite website and found it very intimidating. There is a 97% rejection rate for permits. Over the previous five years, there had been a 400% increase in requests for permits. The movie *Wild* contributed to this increase because the JMT and Pacific Crest Trail (PCT) are the same trail for 150 miles.

I watched *Wild* in the fall of 2015 and was amazed. I had never heard of long-distance thru-hikes and had really never hiked before. Sure, as a kid, we did small hikes, but nothing more than a couple of miles. Long-distance hiking was in a league of its own.

I was born in St. Louis and lived there until I was nine. Then we moved to Florence, Colorado, where we lived briefly before moving to Canon City, Colorado. We lived there until I was 13 and then moved back to St. Louis. My mom was from Colorado, and both of my parents went to college there.

You wouldn't think it with my dad being an accountant, but he is very outdoorsy. While living in Colorado, we camped in tents, went rafting, and took the ski lifts up Pikes Peak during the summer and mountain biked down. We never skied because we didn't have the money for it. But we enjoyed a lot of the outdoors, even though we were *always* underprepared.

For example, my dad decided to go rafting down the Arkansas River, which had large rapids, in a pool raft. For some reason, he thought it would be fine for me, my sister, and her friend to raft the 12 or so miles from Canon City to Florence.

The three of us girls (aged 10–11) each had our own inner tube, and my dad was in a pool raft. We were all tied together with some rope. We almost died many times, including when we hit a huge dam and were close to getting sucked into it. My sister's friend climbed the rocks to the top of the cliff hoping we could all go around the dam, but there was a prison fence there. I was scarred for months after that trip and vowed to pop the inner tubes if they ever tried to go again. They all loved it, while I was terrified.

I am not exactly a daredevil, but I love adventures, and I love challenging myself. I've completed four half-marathons even though I hate running. It's a love-hate relationship, really. I love the way I feel when it's over. However, not breathing well and being in pain is not exactly fun. But it is super fulfilling when you see what you accomplished at the end.

After seeing the movie *Wild*, I was in awe that Cheryl Strayed did not have hiking experience and still completed the Pacific Crest Trail, or PCT. The PCT stretches from Mexico to Canada and is over 2,600 miles. I loved the movie and the endurance she had.

But I had no interest in hiking through the desert and struggling for water. I drink over 100 ounces of water in my everyday life and couldn't imagine being out there with little water, sweating away what water I did have.

During the Pacific Northwest section, it rains a lot. Hiking and camping in the rain also did not sound appealing. To top it off, that trail takes about six months to complete. Working full-time, I knew there was no way I could get that time off.

When Barry told me about the JMT a few months after I saw Wild, I thought, *This is doable. Water is plenty, the temperatures are bearable, there is little rain, and I could complete it in three weeks.* I received three weeks of vacation a year and figured I could save all of my time off. The JMT seemed like a reasonable trail.

I decided to apply for a permit. To get one, you must fax, yes, fax in a request with your top three choices for entry. You also have to request the permit six months in advance. They only allow ten passes from each trailhead per day.

It took me days to figure out this process. I read lots of blogs and bought a book called *Plan & Go, The John Muir Trail*, by Gerret Kalkoffen. It helped tremendously, but the process made me want to pull my hair out. I understand now why people just give up on getting a permit. You'll often hear, "The hardest part of the JMT is getting a permit."

I used a website to send in a fax each day. My top three choices were in the Yosemite Valley area (Happy Isles, Little Yosemite Valley, and Glacier Point). When you get a rejection, they send an email letting you know you were not chosen in the lottery. It's very disheartening to get those emails.

After a week of rejections, I decided to tell Barry I was applying for a permit. You see, Barry was 25, fit, adventurous, and was used to thru-hiking and more extreme sports like mountain biking.

I was 36, about to have surgery for two parathyroid tumors, fit but overweight, and sort of a scaredy-cat. We went to lunch one day, and he mentioned something about wanting to do the JMT. I said, "Permits are hard to get, and you have to get it six months in advance."

Surprised, he asked, "How do you know that?" I replied, "Because I've been looking into it, and I've been faxing in a request for a permit, well, two permits, but I've been rejected every day." I was applying for two permits in case he wanted to go or in case another friend wanted to go. I figured having an experienced hiker with me was a good idea, but requesting more than two permits would limit my chances of being accepted.

On March 16, 2016, I flew from Long Beach, California (where I had been living for 13 years) to Tampa, Florida, to remove two parathyroid tumors. When I got back to the hotel after surgery, I checked my email and was elated when I saw the news: "This confirms your reservation, made on 03/16/2016, for a wilderness permit for the following trip." My start date would be August 31, 2016.

I immediately started to research the trail even more. Going in September meant the temperature would be in the 80's during the day and 30's during the night.

Receiving that permit made it official. There was no turning back for me—it was decided. Now, I needed to prepare.

You Are Not Prepared

I did not have any equipment or gear for backpacking. I also had not really hiked, ever. I certainly had never backpacked before. Tent camping in Missouri and Colorado, where my parents provided everything, wasn't exactly good preparation. I was also overweight and had joined Weight Watchers in January to try and get back into shape. In addition, I was recovering from surgery.

Books

The first book I read was *Plan & Go: The John Muir Trail* by Gerret Kalkorren. This book helped tremendously with understanding the basics, weather, water, food, supplies needed, elevation gains, and his personal experience hiking the trail with a friend. The book helped me get started on what gear I would need.

I also read *Almost Somewhere: Twenty-Eight Days on the John Muir Trail* by Suzanne Roberts. This book was written in 2012, but Suzanne hiked the trail in 1993 with two friends. It was when they were 22 and just graduated college. It was great to read about three women hiking the trail and during a time when women barely hiked it.

There are many more women who hike the JMT now, but men still dominate the trail. Reading about Suzanne's experience was great because she talks about the route, why she hiked it, what challenges she faced, and really painted a picture. I could barely put the book down. I got more and more excited as I read about the adventure.

Movies

I watched *Wild* in the fall of 2015 and re-watched it about a month before I left for the JMT. I like this movie because it highlights that the trail is never just a trail. It's about life.

I watched *High Sierra—A Journey on the John Muir Trail*. This real-life short film follows a group of young guys who hiked the trail in 2011. It was great to see but also worrisome. These are guys in their early 20's, and on day 4, one guy says, "I'm a pretty active, fit guy, and there is no way I could have prepared for this." One guy had to bail around mile 60 because he got sick.

I watched a documentary called *Mile . . . Mile and Half*, which follows a group of people of various age groups and is really well done. The scenery is beautiful, and it just makes you super excited to be out there.

These movies allowed me to prepare for the terrain, the weather, and the challenges. I highly recommend them.

Gear

Shortly after I told my friend Barry that I got two permits, he sent me an email with lots of links to reviews of gear and where to buy top-quality stuff.

I had stepped into an REI for the first time the weekend before he sent the email. I was overwhelmed. I walked around, nervous that people were staring at me, thinking, *What are you doing in here? You're not like us.*

You see, hikers have a distinct look. They wear khaki and earth tones; they're fit, they eat granola, and they love to "live off the land." I was fit but overweight, I like wearing bright colors, and I like non-granola food.

I felt like they all knew I was inexperienced, and I was terrified to tell them I had never backpacked but was going to hike the JMT. I didn't talk to anyone, just browsed around. I left with buying only two things: an REI membership and a National Geographic John Muir Trail pocket guide.

When I got Barry's email with links for the critical stuff (sleeping bags, tents, backpacks), I was relieved. When I told him I had gone to an REI for the first time, he emailed me, "Yeah, I definitely WOULD NOT get a tent, sleeping bag, or backpack at REI. They only carry big brands that are overpriced and too heavy, more aimed at the general consumer market than true backpackers. REI can be good for odds and ends—cookware, light jackets, headlamps, etc., but not the best for essentials."

Barry was a big supporter of USA-made quality camping equipment, and I trusted his opinion. He also sent me links to review sites like Outdoor Gear Lab. This was all very helpful but very overwhelming. There is an incredible amount of information and products out there.

It was helpful to research all the products online because I'm tall, 6'1". It's hard to find gear and clothing when you're a tall woman. I ended up buying a Feathered Friends sleeping bag rated for ten degrees that set me back over $500, but I didn't want to get cold, and it's lightweight.

I got the Double Rainbow Tarptent, the Thermarest air pad, and the Wild Ideas bear canister (bear can). All of my experienced backpacker friends and the blog sites I kept reading said, "If you're a real backpacker, you'll go ultralight." Well, that's easier said than done.

For shoes, I chose trail runners because their soles are like hiking boots, but they have a low profile like running shoes. They were more flexible and lightweight than boots.

I ended up loving REI. I bought my backpack there; after the ultralight-weight pack I bought elsewhere online was way too flimsy. I also purchased countless items from headlamps, jackets, shoes, socks, trekking poles, and food. I felt like I was at REI every other week for the next six months.

Once I got over my own insecurity about people judging me, they were super friendly. They spent so much time walking me through options and differences in gear. I even took a six-hour class that REI offered at a park. About six of us (and the leader) went over all of the basics about backpacking and gear. After the class, I changed my Snow Peak stove to a Jetboil, and I am grateful that I did.

One thing I've been trying to work on is not being self-conscious. Often our own insecurities prevent us from having incredible adventures. I knew I had less than six months to plan and prepare, and it forced me to step out of my comfort zone and ask for help. I got help and advice from coworkers, blogs, friends, books, movies, etc.

I also joined a Facebook group called Ladies of the JMT. This group would serve as a place for constant information that was unbelievably helpful, and it was always encouraging. Hearing the struggles other women were facing made me feel less alone, and there were always great ideas and solutions. This was my "go-to" place for information.

Sweet and Salty

As far as training and getting into shape, I would run about two days a week for three miles each time. I would also go to the gym about two days a week and do elliptical, stairs, and weights. I hiked almost every weekend.

I completed my first hike in March in Runyon Canyon in Hollywood, California. I heard this is where a lot of celebrities hiked and was just over three miles. The inclines and declines were pretty steep in several areas. It's a very dirty, dry, dusty, uneven trail. Most people don't do the whole circuit. I saw a girl in a dress and regular shoes who appeared to be on a date in true Hollywood fashion. It wasn't my crowd, and it was also very crowded. I realized after that hike that I needed trekking poles.

I worked my way up to longer and longer hikes. I hiked Mount Wilson, Crystal Cove, Malibu, Rancho Palos Verde, and Lake Forest. In April, I hiked in Rancho Palos Verde with my sister-in-law, Gabby. We planned on hiking five miles but ended up getting a little lost and climbing back up the wrong mountain.

Because of the wrong turn, we ended up hiking eight miles. The trails in Rancho Palos Verde are beautiful. The entire trail gives you views of the ocean. It's also a challenge as it's pretty steep. There aren't many people on the trail either. Online, it looked like one trail would go to the ocean, but we never found it. I think it was closed off due to erosion.

I hiked a few times with my in-laws on various trails, once with my husband, and a couple of times with friends. I was alone for several of the hikes, which was good preparation. In May, I discovered a trail on Mount Wilson. It's not well known to people (there are other trails on this mountain that are more populated). It is seven and a half miles to the top and about 4,700 feet elevation gain. Then you have to come down the same way you went up, another seven and a half miles down and 4,700 feet descent.

The first time I tried this trail, I only made it to Orchard Camp, which has some rubble of a camp that used to be there. It is three and a half miles to get to Orchard Camp. Doing seven miles roundtrip with that steep of a trail is strenuous.

There is hardly anybody on this trail, which is nice, but it can be a little creepy. For the first two miles, there is no tree cover. Then suddenly you get into a bit of forest. It's beautiful, provides shade, and feels like you entered another world, far away from Los Angeles.

The second time I hiked this mountain, there were heat warnings. I had to get my hikes in, so I completed it anyway. It was Father's day, and my friend Valerie went with me. We started in the morning and had a snack when we made it to Orchard Camp. The mosquitos and bugs were crazy and wouldn't leave us alone. Every time we stopped to take a small break, they would swarm. Even while hiking, we would constantly be swatting them away.

I knew it would be a hot day, so I brought a hydration bladder containing 50 ounces of water. I also had a water belt with two bottles of water, each carrying nine ounces. While we quickly ate a snack at Orchard Camp, we chatted with a man and his son.

The man warned us that the next section is very steep, but there is a bench about two miles up. We already thought the trail was steep, so we were a little worried. We continued, but the tree cover disappeared, and the heat intensified. We kept asking each other about turning back, but we're stubborn and didn't want to be the person who turned around.

The plan was to hike to the top, which we thought was 12 miles roundtrip. When we realized it would be 15 miles roundtrip, we decided we'd make it to the bench and turn around. However, the heat became overwhelming, and we were just about out of water. We agreed to turn around, about .7 miles away from the bench.

As we headed back down, we were quickly out of water. We had tree cover again for a few miles, but the last two miles had no tree cover. It's on the east side of the mountain, so the sun had been heating the ground all day.

It was almost 11:00 am, and Valerie and I were

almost in heatstroke. Valerie stopped talking and was practically running down the mountain in an attempt to get back to our cars as fast as possible.

The sun was blazing, and we could see houses at the bottom that had pools. We joked about how much we wanted to jump into those pools. I stopped sweating and began getting goosebumps. I knew that wasn't good. The only other time that happened to me was at mile ten of a half marathon that I did and got overheated. After finishing that marathon, I almost passed out.

Not only was I not sweating, but there was also salt all over my face and arms that I could feel and see. There was almost nobody around, and the sun was beating on us.

When we got back down, we sat in my car and turned on the air conditioner. I had two bottles of coconut water in a lunch pail. Valerie had never tried coconut water before. I gave her a bottle, and we both drank it as fast as possible. We didn't say a word—just drank nonstop until the bottles were gone.

Valerie said, "I don't think I'd normally like the taste of coconut water, but right now, it tastes amazing." I checked the weather, and the temperature was 106°F with a "real feel" of 113°F! I do not recommend hiking in scorching temperatures.

I had some hot water in my car but figured I would stop at a nearby gas station for water and a snack. I stopped at a 7-Eleven and bought a Slurpee, large water, and a snack tray of fruit, almonds, cheese, and meat. I drank that Slurpee so fast that I kept getting a brain freeze.

I was craving grapes, and they tasted like heaven. Valerie also stopped at a gas station and bought a gallon of water, and drank it all the way home. Both of us drank the extremely hot water we had in our car on the way to the gas station. That's when you know you just need water.

From that experience, I learned I need salt pills. When I sweat for long periods, especially in extreme heat, I lose salt. A lot of people are salty sweaters—about 30%.

How do you know if you are a salty sweater? You can literally see and feel the salt on your body. The good thing is that REI sells salt pills. You take one every 20–60 minutes of exercise. I take them when I'm sweating a lot, and they really help. The salt is replenishing your electrolytes, which you need for the water to penetrate your cells.

You'd think I would have learned to carry more water and food while doing all-day hikes. But sometimes, I learn the hard way.

At the end of July, I hiked a trail in Malibu. I knew it was going to be hot, but I couldn't start early that day. I started in the afternoon and planned to hike ten miles. I had my 50-ounce hydration bladder and water belt with two bottles carrying nine ounces each. I also had a power bar, and a small packet of what tastes like apple sauce, which is designed to replenish sugar during workouts.

After about four miles, I ate the power bar. The section where I was supposed to turn had a gate blocking it, so I ended up going up and then back down another mountain, which added a total of four miles to my hike.

I got back to the gate and realized I just had to go around it. The heat started to be a little overwhelming because there was no shade at all.

I was climbing down into a ravine and was trying to save my water, but it was too hot. The trail was so steep; I was sweating like crazy. I ate the apple sauce packet, but as I climbed out of the ravine, I started to feel pretty weak. I hadn't seen anybody in about four hours. The trail was just going and going and going, climbing up. It was a long, straight incline trail on the side of the mountain.

All of a sudden, a super fit man in his 60's was running down the mountain. I looked at him and asked, "Am I almost to the top?" He said, "Not really. Are you okay?" I'm sure I looked like a maniac.

I said I was okay but was just super hot. The man asked how much water I had left, and I told him about five ounces. He said, "That's not enough. Here, take mine." He had pear juice in two bottles, each about 16 ounces.

I told him I didn't want to take his water because he needed it. He insisted and gave me a bottle. The man explained, "I've seen too many people get into trouble on these trails. It's really confusing at the top. Here, I'll go run back up and mark the trail that you need to turn off with an arrow made of rocks."

After the second turnaround, he would go left, but I would need to go right to get back to my car. He said he lived in the area and wanted to know how I knew of the trails there. He didn't want me telling anybody about the site as he liked that they were so empty.

This man also gave me his cell phone number and told me to text him when I got back to my car (and got cell service), so he knows that I made it back okay. He instructed me to leave his water bottle behind the entrance sign. He said, "You have to start carrying more water and sugar. You're replacing your salt, but you also need to replace your sugar."

The man ran up the mountain, and I continued to slug along. I saw his first arrow directing me through dry, low brush. I was grateful the trail leveled off a bit. Then there was a second arrow. I was winding on a narrow path halfway covered in brush that I would not have found if it were not for him.

I saw a parking lot in the distance and was elated! Then as I got closer, I realized my car was in the other parking lot . . . on the other side of the small mountain. I climbed up and down again and finally made it to my car. I ended up hiking 15 miles that day. I left the man's bottle behind the sign as he instructed and included a $20 bill in it for his help and generosity.

I texted him to let him know that I was back. The next day he texted, thanking me for the $20 and saying it wasn't necessary. But in my honor, he'd take it to REI and buy something for himself. Later, I googled his name, and it turns out he was a long-time successful producer in Hollywood. I will always appreciate his kindness and help that day.

This hike taught me I really need more water, and I also needed sugar. I bought a bigger hydration bladder, 70 ounces. I also started to carry more sugary food items on hikes.

I was determined to make it to the top of Mount Wilson, so on the fourth of July (American Independence), I started in the morning, carrying enough water and snacks.

It was tough, but at the very least, I wanted to make it to that bench that Valerie and I just barely missed. I ate a snack at Orchard Camp and started the steeper section of the trail.

I climbed, huffing and puffing along the way. Suddenly, a bee stung me on the forehead! The pain immediately hit me. I tried to look up and couldn't see the bee. Then I put my hand on my forehead and felt the bee squirming around. I freaked out and knocked the bee off of my forehead. He fell to the ground, where I stepped on him.

I could feel the stinger still stuck to my head but couldn't see it to pull it out. I frantically started running up the mountain. I hadn't seen anybody in hours, but I desperately hoped I'd find someone to help me.

Within a minute, a couple in their 30s appeared who were climbing down. They could tell that I was panicked and asked if they could help me. I explained what happened, and the woman said, "The stinger is in your forehead. Do you want me to pull it out?" I screamed, "Yes!"

The woman pulled the stinger out, and I was in a lot of pain. I explained that I had been stung by a bee a few years earlier on my inner upper arm, and it swelled up so bad that I had to go to urgent care. The doctor explained that I'm allergic to bee stings, and each time I'm stung, the reaction will worsen.

I debated on what to do, but climbing down would be much farther than climbing up. The couple told me that the top had a parking lot and a few buildings, so maybe I could hitch a ride from someone.

I decided to keep climbing, and the sting burned for about an hour. I didn't seem to be having an anaphylactic reaction, so I figured that I had some time before the sting got worse.

Eventually, I made it to the bench! I sat down to take a break and look at the views. It was about another two miles to the top, and I continued climbing.

I reached the top after climbing for seven and a half miles straight. I was exhausted. There were cars at the top and people picnicking at tables. I refilled my water at a pump and walked around. There was an observatory that I walked around. After a snack, I decided that I wanted to hike back down instead of asking for help. I finally made it to the top, and I needed to train for downhill climbing too.

I made it down and crashed that evening with complete exhaustion while fireworks exploded out the window. I hiked 15 miles and climbed up 4,700 feet and back down 4,700 feet.

Over the next few days, my forehead swelled more and more until it looked like I had bad plastic surgery. One eye was much smaller than the other. Barry, my coworker, came around my cubicle and said, "Wow! You really are allergic to bee stings! You look deformed."

I went to urgent care and got medicine and steroids. It took ten days for the swelling to go down, which is typical. My primary care doctor gave me an epi-pen in case this happened again. If I got stung on the neck, it would make my throat swell. I could also have an anaphylactic reaction in the future, and the epi-pen would slow the reaction until I could reach a hospital. The pen was heavy, but I decided to carry the two-pack with me on the JMT in case I was stung again. When I was 17, I had an anaphylactic reaction to allergy shots and almost died en route to the hospital, so I felt better bringing the epi-pen with me.

Testing Equipment

At the beginning of August, I went on a weekend-long camping trip to Idyllwild, California, with a small group of people from my church. I had seen announcements for a camping trip throughout the previous few years but had never gone. My husband wasn't much of a camper. When I saw the trip was one month before I left for the JMT, I thought it would be a perfect time to try out all of my gear.

I had to leave that Friday afternoon after work, and it's about a three-hour drive with traffic. The group leader, Patty, asked me if I could pick up another girl, Debbie, and bring her with me because she needed a ride. It turns out Debbie lived about two miles from me and is only two years younger. It was great to have a car mate to keep me company during the drive. We discovered we have a lot in common, and she goes hiking and backpacking too.

When we arrived at the campsite, it was 9:00 pm and dark. Idyllwild is beautiful, and it was my first time there. Everyone else was already set up. I was sharing a site with another family since my tent was so small. The campsites were nice but relatively cramped.

There wasn't any grass at the sites, but there were giant redwood trees. I set up my tent next to a tree. My campsite had a family of four, with two kids that were five and nine. The kids were sweet and tried to help me set up in the dark. Patty and Debbie also helped. There were about 30 people there from the church at the surrounding campsites.

It was a bit embarrassing setting up my tent for the second time. The first time setting it up was in my backyard, and I had never slept in it. Patty was telling everyone I was about to hike the JMT. I was afraid they were all thinking, *How are you going to backpack for three weeks when you don't even know how to set up your tent?* However, I was pleasantly surprised that they were all so nice.

I got my tent, sleeping bag, and sleeping pad all set up using a headlamp. Everyone else was car camping, and either had a camper or a large family-sized tent. There were restrooms nearby with showers too. I kept hearing, "You're sleeping in that? But it's so small." Patty would chime in and say, "She's hiking the JMT, and she's trying out all her gear." It made me feel proud and supported.

That night, I felt excited and more confident in being able to backpack for three weeks alone. I slept okay, but I was on a slight incline, and my sleeping bag kept sliding off my sleeping pad. I also had a blow-up pillow that was pretty big and wouldn't fit inside the hood of my sleeping bag and kept sliding out from under my head.

I woke up a lot that night because of all of the slipping

and sliding. I didn't fall asleep until around midnight because I just couldn't sleep. I was also a little hot. The overnight lows were in the high 50's, and my sleeping bag was rated for ten degrees.

At 6:00 am, the sun came shining into camp. The family in my campsite kept walking from their truck to the picnic table and would trip on one of my strings that were holding up my tent. My tent had one pole, and it went straight down the middle. It was a rectangle shape, with enough room to sleep two people.

If two people were to sleep in there, you would not be able to fit anything else. I chose this tent because it's lightweight and made for taller people. I could actually sit up in the tent, but barely. Since my tent only had one pole, it had six strings staked into the ground to hold it up. Each corner had a stake, and the two sides had a stake.

Each side of the tent had a door with a rain flap. After about the seventh time that the family tripped on my brand new stakes, I politely asked if they would stop hitting my tent, so it doesn't break. It's very delicate since it's lightweight. I was worried my tent would fall apart before I even hit the trail.

For breakfast, I used my brand new Jetboil and cooked a dehydrated egg breakfast. I couldn't help but think of the REI instructor of the class I took. He said, "Make sure you don't show up backpacking with items that still have tags on them. You need to make sure you use your equipment before you hit the trail to make sure it all works."

I laughed, thinking, *Great, I'm the person with all the*

tags. But it's okay; this is my trip to try it all out. I also made myself a Starbucks latte that came with cream, sugar, and coffee all in one. All I had to do was boil water. My Jetboil was my bowl, and I had a foldable cup for my coffee. I also had a spork. It was all I planned on taking with me on the JMT, so I figured I better do it as I would on the trail for practice.

Everyone else had amazing eggs and bacon on their grill. The family sharing the campsite shared some bacon with me, and it was delicious. I still ate my dehydrated meal but couldn't pass up the bacon.

The afternoon plans consisted of a minimal hike and then a swim in the pool. There were primarily families except for Debbie and me. The kids couldn't do a long hike. Debbie hiked often, so we decided to drive down the mountain a few miles to a trail that would take us to Suicide Rock.

The trial was about eight miles roundtrip. It was beautiful, and the views at the top were breathtaking. We enjoyed lunch at the top and soaked up the warm sun. Debbie is a petite redhead with a fire inside that is contagious. She has a genuine care for people, and I was thrilled to have her there for the hike.

When we got back from the hike, I ate my dehydrated meal (risotto) but did not enjoy it. I was trying out all of my equipment and gear, but since it was a car camping trip, I also brought my big red cooler. I had loaded it with orange juice, grapes, strawberries, potato salad, and a dessert.

I knew there would be a potluck Saturday evening and didn't want to be empty-handed. I posted a picture of my tent (with the cooler next to it) on Facebook, and my friend Dave commented, "If you pull that big red cooler behind you on the JMT, it'll make it a lot harder for you, BUT you'd be the most popular person on the whole trail! ;)" It still makes me laugh to picture myself pulling along a cooler on the trail.

I participated in the potluck since my dehydrated meal was not appetizing. It was a great evening sitting around the fire. I slept much better that night.

The following day we all got together for some pancakes that Patty made, and I brought strawberries and orange juice. I figured I had already tried out my gear, and I could enjoy a real breakfast. The whole trip was so fun. It got me out of my comfort zone, and I made new friends. Plus, trying out all of my gear was a must, and it was nice to do it around supportive people where I also still had some amenities nearby.

I realized all of the slipping and sliding in the tent was because I forgot to seal my tent. When I got home, I ordered the glue to seal it. The sealant helps keep the rain out, and in addition to putting it on the tent's seams, you put stripes on the floor. The sealant prevents all the sliding.

Once the sealant arrived, I set my tent up, watched the YouTube video, and went to work. It was pretty easy, but I needed to let it dry before putting it away. I also realized I did not like the pillow I had because it was too inflated and too big, which is why it kept popping out from under my head. Instead, I ordered a pillow from Feathered Friends that is down feather and folds into itself.

The trip also made me realize my backpack was too flimsy. I only used it to store items during that trip, but it would just collapse when I set it down. I also knew I didn't have all of my gear in there, including my bear can, and there is no way it would all fit. I ended up returning the lightweight backpack for a more durable Osprey.

I only had about three weeks before leaving for the JMT, and I went into REI on a mission to find the right backpack. The Huntington Beach REI has a limited selection in stock, so I drove to Orange, California, where their inventory is much more extensive.

An employee helped me determine one that would work for me. Being 6'1", I knew most women's backpacks wouldn't fit me well. I ended up trying a men's Osprey. The employee loaded the pack with about 25 pounds of sandbags to wear around the store and feel it with weight.

I wandered around the store for about an hour with that pack on while I shopped for other items I still needed. I had lost 30 pounds in the last six months, so I waited to buy clothes until it got closer to my start date.

Being tall and a little overweight makes it difficult to find clothes. I guess the companies that make the clothes think all hikers are short and petite? I couldn't find pants that would fit, and my rain jacket and down jacket were from the men's department. My shoes were also from the men's section.

I bought my shoes a couple of months before to break them in, and I happened to go during their "biggest sale of the year." The store was jam-packed, and I was there for a couple of hours trying on and walking around in several different shoes. I kept reading that you should buy one to two sizes larger because your feet will swell with all the walking, and if there isn't enough space, you'll get black toenails (or lose your toenail).

I wear a size 12 in women's shoes, which is hard enough to find. There was no way any store would have a size 13–14. I turned to men's shoes but had to keep trying different shoes because if I had enough space for the toes, the heel would come off. If you're reading this and work for a company that sells clothing or shoes for hiking, please start selling additional sizes.

So, back to walking around the store with my backpack filled with 25 pounds. This was actually really helpful because I could get a sense of how it would adjust to my body. Usually, I would have been really embarrassed to be walking around the store with this backpack for an hour but knowing I had a deadline and would be out there alone for three weeks gave me the courage to be a little embarrassed.

Two weeks before I started the JMT, I hiked with my backpack with about 20 pounds. I hiked Mount Wilson to Orchard Camp (seven miles round trip with about 2,500-feet elevation gain and descent).

The weekend before I left for the JMT, I added weight, and it was around 40 pounds. I quickly realized hiking with a heavy pack makes a huge difference. The weight on the shoulders and hips can be overwhelming. I also felt it in the legs. Each step to climb up took a toll. Going downhill, I had to be careful not to let it pull me down.

Two days before I left for the JMT, I did my last hike. I had my backpack filled to around 40 pounds and hiked Crystal Cove in Orange County. I was about half-way into the hike, going uphill, sweating and panting. All of a sudden, a girl came up from behind me. She also had a large backpack.

I took off my headphones, and we laughed about how we were the only ones with these large packs. She was a spunky, petite girl with short blond hair. Her name was Mandy. I told her that I was training for the JMT, and she told me she was preparing for the Trans-Catalina Trail. It's a trail that is 37 miles and goes all around Catalina Island, which is a small island off the coast of California.

Mandy and I chatted for about 20 minutes, but then she had to take a different trail to get back to her car. She was super positive and friendly, and it was encouraging to meet someone so supportive. I found her on Facebook, and we've been able to connect about our hiking adventures. We even spent four days backpacking together in Olympic National Forest two years later.

Too Much/Not Enough

Planning what you're going to eat for three weeks hiking through the Sierra Mountains is a challenge, to say the least. I read about different food options in books. For example, in *Almost Somewhere: Twenty-Eight Days on the John Muir Trail*, the author talked about not having enough food.

They would only have a few tablespoons of oatmeal in the morning, and they were always hungry and running out of food. You don't want to run out of food, but you also don't want to carry too much food or carry heavy food.

Dehydrated meals are popular. Some people do this themselves, but I didn't have a dehydrator, and I also don't have patience for that. You can buy the food already packaged, but it's expensive. There are also options like beef jerky, peanut butter, tortillas, and mashed potatoes.

I had been gluten-free for several months leading up to the JMT. Several doctors have told me that I am allergic and should be avoiding wheat. But it's tough to avoid it altogether. And it's delicious. It does inflame my joints and upsets my stomach, so I had been avoiding wheat/gluten for months and planned on only packing gluten-free foods. This was a challenge when most people load up on certain carbs, like tortillas. I couldn't, so I figured I'd do mostly rice-based dinners for the carbs. After lots and lots of researching and reading about various food options, here's where I landed with food.

- Breakfast: oatmeal, raisins, brown sugar, or powdered eggs. It was mainly oatmeal. I wasn't sure how I'd like the powdered eggs, so I only had eggs a few times.
- Snack: Protein shake or protein powder
- Lunch: Tuna packet in a plastic pouch, dried meats like jerky or salami, cheese, almonds
- Snack: Almonds, peanut butter, fruit strip, apple sauce-type packet
- Dinner: Freeze-dried meal, chocolate bits

I also had these little exercise waffles made by Stinger. They're so delicious and designed for giving you sugar and carbs while exercising. They make a gluten-free version as well. These became my favorite foods that I looked forward to each day. I had a couple of chocolate bars that I could break into little squares. It would only last for a couple of days, and I ended up wishing I had more.

The thing that makes you want to pull your hair while preparing your food is the amount of time you spend prepping it. The freeze-dried meals come in large

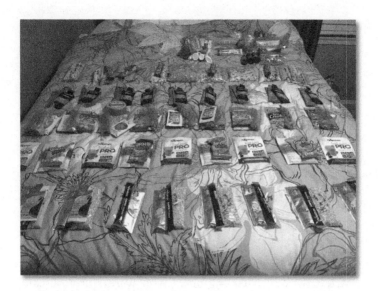

plastic bags, and they'll take up too much space in the bear can.

If you're not familiar with a bear can, it's required in the Sierras to keep bears and humans safe. Back in the day, you could hang your food in a bag from a tree. You don't want to keep any food at your campsite; it needs to be 100 feet away in case a bear tries to get it.

The problem with using a tree to hang your food is when you don't have a suitable tree (or a tree at all) nearby, you can't hang it. People also weren't doing a great job at hanging it correctly, and bears would send their cubs to climb the tree and get the food. Once a bear gets food, he'll keep trying when he sees it. Bears can smell food (or anything with a scent) a mile away.

The bears in the Sierras are black bears, and thankfully, they're afraid of humans. They stay away for the most part, but if they get human food, they can become aggressive because they'll associate humans with food.

If they become aggressive, they usually have to be put down. The bears are now used to seeing the bear cans and they often don't even bother attempting to open them.

The law in most of the Sierra Mountains is that you must carry a bear canister. They're specifically designed to keep bears out. They're cylinders, and you either have to open them by pressing the lid in as you turn it (think medicine bottle), or there are little levers, and you need a coin to turn them. After lots of research, I ordered a custom-size bear can from Wild Ideas Bearikade. They're a small business in the USA, and the company was started by aerospace engineers who were able to create the lightest weight bear cans that are also the toughest. They don't have the twist open, which I liked because I had read reviews of people saying the twist top (like a medicine bottle) was challenging to open in the cold.

I didn't want to struggle to get my food, and Wild Ideas makes the lightest one on the market. The only problem is the price. They had three sizes, and all were 9″ in diameter. The small was 8″ tall, the medium was 10.5″ tall, and the large was 14.5″ tall. I thought the large was too tall, so I ordered a custom one that was 12.5″ tall. I'm glad I did because a taller one would have been hard to fit in my backpack with everything else I had.

It set me back around $325 and took three to four weeks to make. The company, Wild Ideas, now has a fourth size, and it's 12″ tall. Their website says, "New, by popular demand: The Bearikade Blazer is the choice for fast hikers on longer trips. If used as a personal unit, it can supply you for up to 9 days with efficient packing."

My bear canister didn't arrive until about a week before I left for the JMT, so I was only able to hike with it once before leaving.

There are a few options of places you can mail yourself food and supplies in advance, so you don't have to carry so much. I decided to mail myself two resupply buckets while on the JMT. I sent one to Red's Meadow at mile 60 and one to Muir Trail Ranch at mile 105. My bear can could only hold a maximum of 9 days' worth of food. Remember, you also have to put anything with a scent in it too.

There is no resupply point from Muir Trail Ranch to Mount Whitney, so that meant I'd have to hike 115+ miles in nine days. There are a couple of post offices you can use, but they're off the trail. The shortest one is six miles each way. I'd rather hike quicker than have to hike an extra 12 miles to get more food. You can also hire a mule runner to deliver your food to you on the trail. However, they're expensive, and it's tough to coordinate since there is no cell service in the mountains.

Prepping the food was incredibly exhausting. I had to ship it out three weeks before leaving for the JMT to ensure it would arrive in time. The resupply drop points make you ship it in a five-gallon plastic bucket because rats and other animals can chew through cardboard. I didn't have my bear can yet, so I had to hope it would all fit. I figured if it didn't fit in a five-gallon bucket, it surely wouldn't fit in my bear can.

I went to multiple stores to buy the food: REI, Target, Sprouts, etc. I spent several hours sorting the freeze-dried meals into smaller zip-top bags. Each freeze-dried bag I purchased was 2 or 2½ servings, so I divided it up into single servings. The problem was most single servings were only around 300 calories, with some being 400 calories. I tried to throw in some sides like mashed potatoes, but I didn't have much room in my bear can.

I laid it all out on the bed and sorted it by meal. I had read that people tended to get sick of the same foods, so you should vary it. That sounds good in theory, but it's already so much work that it was just easier to pack the same foods in each resupply bucket and my initial bear can.

As I laid it all out, it looked like too much food and not enough at the same time. The day before I was going to ship it out, I saw a post on the Ladies of the JMT Facebook page about cheeses that World Market sells. They don't need to be refrigerated, and they have lots of flavors. Initially, I didn't have any cheese because I thought that was gross because they couldn't be refrigerated. I heard of some people who were sending themselves Babybel cheese, but that seemed strange to me.

I headed to World Market and picked up several cheese triangles and some meats (salami and prosciutto). This worked out well. They were fancy cheeses and meats, were smoked, and didn't need to be refrigerated. It was like the stuff you see at Hickory Farms.

I tried to load the food by day, so I wouldn't have to dig around. This didn't work out because it created too many empty gaps. I had to repack it all by like-items. Items need to be next to objects of the same size to be compacted correctly.

I quickly realized my two 5-gallon buckets were full.

I had to remove a few items, and it really worried me. If I couldn't fit my food in this colossal bucket, how would it fit in my bear can? I also threw in a few treats in my resupplies that I could devour when I picked it up, like wine. In addition to food, I also added some blister pads, new socks, a razor, and other first-aid type items.

I headed to the post office and mailed my resupply buckets. The guy at the post office looked at me with curiosity. It was nerve-racking knowing if I forgot something in my resupply, it was too late.

About a week after I mailed my buckets, I realized I forgot to include pads. Yes, women have to worry about these things. I figured I'd be starting my period around the middle of the trip. Since I would be staying at Muir Trail Ranch (105 miles into the trail), I mailed a large envelope of pads. To mail buckets, it costs around $75. But you could also send envelopes for no charge.

When my bear can arrived, I had a hard time fitting all my food in it. I took out some snickers bars I had and only kept 2–3. I took out a few more items and tried to reduce any extra air in the zip-top bags. It was crazy how fast that thing filled up.

Last Bit of Comfort

Preparing to be gone from your everyday life for three weeks is exhausting. I had to prepare at work and make sure everything was complete. I was the Recruiting Manager, and thankfully, we weren't hiring at the moment, and I was just working on projects. I also had to pay all my bills in advance so I wouldn't miss a deadline.

In May 2016 (four months before I left for the JMT), I asked my husband of nine years to move out. I loved him very much, but he had lied one too many times, and I couldn't trust him. He didn't want to move out, and I struggled with the thought of him being gone, but I needed space to think about what I wanted long-term.

He moved into the guest room instead. This was hard and confusing, so in July, I asked him to move out again, and he moved into his mom's house. With him not living at our house, I needed to make sure someone would check on my cat, the house, and get the mail. He agreed to stop by and do these things while I was away. I saw him about two weeks before I left for the trip. It wasn't easy because we didn't know what the future would hold.

My cousin, Misty, considered hiking the JMT with me or at least a section. She lived in Atlanta and just finished her graduate degree in school counseling and would likely start a new job during that time, so she couldn't be away that long.

About three weeks before I left, I posted on Facebook saying I had an extra permit to hike the JMT and wanted to see if anybody wanted to use it. My friend, Dave, hiked the JMT in 2012 in seven days. Yes, seven days. He was doing about 30 miles a day, didn't have a tent (just had a sleeping bag), didn't cook (only ate bars and stuff), and powered through. He's the guy that does iron man races and extreme biking races. Dave was around 40 years old and was super fit. He owned a mountain bike shop in Woodland Hills, California. He said he'd take the other permit, but he would need to finish in ten days to be back at his shop.

I went to work on Monday and wrapped up everything. My coworkers were all very supportive and excited to hear about the trip when I returned. I was off work on Tuesday, August 30th, and spent the day getting everything ready. I weighed my pack with a luggage scale, and it said 50 pounds (with complete food and water). Dave, his girlfriend, and I planned to drive up to Lone Pine separately.

Lone Pine is a small town just below Mount Whitney. Dave had arranged to leave his car at the museum in town for a small fee. They didn't have enough space for me there, so I got a spot at the golf course. It was around

$90 for three weeks. Dave's girlfriend couldn't leave LA until 4:00 pm because of school. We decided to meet at the golf course around 8:30 pm.

I was in such a hurry that day to get everything mailed out, make sure I had everything I needed, and make certain the house was in order. I didn't have time for dinner, so I stopped through a McDonald's drive-through on the way out of town. Gluten-free, out the window. I really enjoyed a burger and fries. I thought, *It's okay because I'll need the energy.*

Los Angeles traffic is some of the worst traffic in the country. It should have taken me 4 hours to get to Lone Pine. The traffic was so bad; my GPS routed me through Angeles National Forest. I spent about 90 minutes weaving through the mountains. Then finally, I got to a straight highway and I was on my way.

I passed a beautiful wind farm as the sun was setting. I was nervous but felt ready. I arrived at the golf course around 9:00 pm, and Dave and his girlfriend (Ivana) met me there. I left a check in the slot and jumped into Ivana's new white Civic. We wanted to stay the night in Mammoth Lakes since it was closer to Yosemite Valley. It would be another two-hour drive to Mammoth, so Ivana slept in the back with their large Pitbull that was along for the ride.

Dave and I used to work together years before. He was the Sales Director, and I was an individual contributor at the time. Dave had been four levels of management above me. We didn't interact much at work, but I always thought he was interesting.

Life is funny. Six years after he left the company, here

we were driving up to hike the JMT. We only worked together for about two to three years, and he left the company to open up his bike shop.

A few months before the JMT, there was a reunion of ex-managers. My friend Toni invited me even though I only knew a couple of people. I talked to Dave, and he had given me all sorts of advice about the JMT since he had completed it a few years earlier.

On the drive up, it was clear we didn't know each other well, other than through Facebook. I didn't know how long he and Ivana had been dating or how they met. I knew he used to be married to a woman we used to work with, but they divorced (and she also left the company).

It was nice to chat while driving through the dark highway, surrounded by mountains on both sides. We talked about our plans for the JMT and supplies.

We arrived at the Westin in Mammoth Lakes, where we had reservations. We didn't check in until around 11:00 pm. Dave and I had to pick up the permits in Yosemite Valley by 10:00 am the following day (unless we notified them of a later pick-up). They opened at 8:00 am, and I knew it would probably take another two hours to get to the Valley from Mammoth Lakes.

We both got our room keys, and Dave said, "So, meet in the lobby at 5:30 am? I want to get to the office right at 8:00 am to get permits." I gulped. "Sure, 5:30 am, sounds good."

I got to my room and thought, *WTF? 5:30 am? This is my last night in a bed for three weeks, and I'm going to get around five hours of sleep? Ugh.*

Our permit said we had to make it to at least the Yosemite Valley backpacker campground the first night. That was only five miles from the start, but it was over 2,000 feet ascending in those five miles. I planned on taking my time the first half since my reservations for Muir Trail Ranch weren't until the 11–12th.

I also read that it can be hard to adjust to the altitude, and many people struggle the first three days. So, I figured I'd plan for that and take it slow at first. Since Dave needed to finish in ten days, he planned on sleeping close to Tuolumne Meadows . . . 22 miles into the trail. His girlfriend was dropping us off at the start of the trailhead, so I couldn't complain.

Have you ever been to a Westin? They are some of the most beautiful hotels around. Dave suggested it because "You'll want a really comfortable bed for your last night in a bed for a while." The Westin in Mammoth Lakes is gorgeous; right in the mountains, log cabin-feel, but elegant. I showered and slept in a T-shirt and underwear since I didn't want to be in my warm thermals. It's strange being at a hotel with a backpack and only essentials. I didn't have my purse or make-up or my toiletries—just backpacking stuff. This definitely wasn't a vacation.

Day

1

It's Go Time

I woke up at 5:10 am and started to pack up, taking my time. I didn't realize it, but the clock in my room was 15 minutes behind, so I was five minutes late meeting Dave and still had to get ready. I texted him that I'd be right down (I had to grab some in-room coffee). I threw on my bright green shirt and black spandex shorts. Dave pulled up the car, and I needed to check out.

Nobody was awake at this hour. I stopped by the desk on the way out to check out, and the woman said, "You didn't check in until after 11:00 pm last night. Here, I'll wave the resort fee for you." That was very nice of her since I didn't get to use any of the resort. I was off to a great start!

We took off as the sun was starting to rise. The views were incredible, and it felt like nobody was awake. Ivana was sleeping in the back.

Dave and I talked about hiking and our experiences at work. I hadn't told Dave about my husband. It felt too personal. Every time I would talk about it to someone, I would end up crying. So, I just avoided it.

The thing is, when you're married, people wonder why you're hiking for three weeks without your husband. I had gotten the blank look from many people before I left. Some people directly asked me. One guy at work, Chris, asked me, "You're married right? Your husband is okay with you going alone?" I just responded, "Yeah, he knows I do my own thing most of the time if something is stuck in my head." Which was also true. He knew if I was determined to do something, there wasn't much he could do to stop me.

When you're married and going on a solo back-packing trip, everyone wonders what's going on. It's hard because you know they're thinking it, but it's not exactly something you want to unload on a coworker or acquaintance.

People assume there's more to a long-distance hike. Some people would say, "This must be a great experience to find yourself." Others would directly ask, "Why are you doing this?" I struggled to articulate why. I would usually say something like, "This is the perfect trail. There's enough water that you don't have to worry about running out, it barely rains, and I can do it in three weeks. And why not?" I couldn't quite put into words why I needed to do this. But I did.

Dave and I chatted about the trail and the differences in our gear. Since he only needed to carry three to four days' worth of food at a time, his pack was much smaller than mine. It made me feel embarrassed when I had to load it into the backseat of his girlfriend's car. I said,

"You're going to be averaging 22–23 miles a day, and I'll average 10–11 miles a day."

Dave responded, "Really, it's harder for you. You have to survive in the wilderness for three weeks. The hard part is setting up camp, cooking food, all of that. I don't have to set up a tent or cook food. I also only have to survive for ten days and only carry food for a few days at a time."

I know he was likely just trying to make me feel better, but I actually think it's true. Part of what makes this trip so hard is the mental wear and tear. Being out there for three weeks is not easy. It's a lot of work to care for yourself that long. I needed to carry more food and supplies than Dave did.

Dave told me about his bike shop. He was well-educated and had a high-level position at the company we worked at together. He decided that he'd rather do something he enjoyed, and he loved being outdoors and active. The bike shop was his perfect solution. He lived in a converted loft just above the shop. Dave said, "I'll never be a millionaire or rich, but I can live the way I want."

I told Dave that I was starting to struggle with an office environment day in and day out. It felt like I was living for the weekends or my few weeks of vacation a year. It didn't seem like it was the best way to live— inside a cubicle. Dave said, "Careful now; you're starting to think like a free person."

We arrived at the permit office at 8:05 am. First, we used the restrooms, the last actual restroom we'd see for a long time.

There were just a couple of people inside. One of the park rangers talked to us for 10–15 minutes about Leave

No Trace (LNT) and all the rules. She showed us a graph of the increase in people hiking the trail over the last several years, compared to the number of permits issued.

I asked her why the lines were different (shouldn't the number of permits equal the number of people who hike the JMT?). The ranger got flustered and tried to think of an answer but couldn't. She looked all around the chart for more information, including the back. I said, "That's fine." She replied, "Let's not get bogged down by this," and continued with her instructions.

As we were walking out of the office, Dave laughed and said, "That was such a McMaster-Carr moment. Explain your data that doesn't make sense. You had her flustered for a good minute." It was a classic McMaster-Carr moment (where we worked). We criticize and critique without even realizing we're doing it.

Once we had our permits, we quickly set off. Dave wanted to hike about 20 miles that day and wanted to start at Happy Isles. My permits were for starting at Glacier Point. Glacier Point is 3,000 feet above Happy Isles. They're basically at the same place, but Happy Isles is at 4,034 feet, and Glacier Point is just above the trail at 7,214 feet.

Happy Isles is the official start to the JMT, and Dave wanted to start there. I'm a bit of a rule follower, and I hesitated. I didn't want our permits taken away. He said, "Let's just go see if there are rangers around and if there are, we'll drive up to Glacier Point."

Happy Isles was a short car drive down the road, but it would take a couple of hours to get to the top of Glacier point by car. We parked the car near the entrance to

Happy Isles. There wasn't a ranger in sight. We agreed to start there.

We started to get our gear ready (backpacks, trekking poles, hats). I quickly ate a beef jerky stick since I hadn't eaten breakfast. I felt very rushed as Dave was pretty much ready, and Ivana's car was illegally parked (there were no spaces left). My pack didn't feel right, but I started walking so I wouldn't fall behind.

It was about half a mile to the trailhead, and I followed behind Dave and Ivana. They were talking and

holding hands, preparing for being apart for the next ten days. When we arrived at the trailhead entry, we took a picture together and one by ourselves.

Ivana said her goodbyes and left. Dave and I started hiking together. The trail begins with a steep incline and is paved. There were a few day-hikers on the trail. Dave was going so fast, and I wanted to take pictures. After about a quarter of a mile, I told Dave we should part ways because I only needed to hike five miles, and I planned on taking it slow. He agreed, and we said our goodbyes.

Shortly after he left, I took off my pack to readjust. The lid of the backpack was completely crooked and almost hanging off. I adjusted it, and it felt much better. I also didn't have time earlier to put on sunscreen or bug spray. I applied both and felt ready.

I brought my iPod shuffle and put my headphones on. I know some people say they only want to hear nature. For me, music inspires my soul and enhances every experience. I need music. It takes me to another world sometimes, and other times, it enhances the world around me. When I would stop for breaks, I would turn it off, but otherwise, I used that iPod every single day.

As I climbed higher and higher, there were fewer and fewer people. The trail was only paved for a little while, maybe a mile. I crossed a bridge over a small river pretty early on, and it seemed most tourists hiked to that spot, took pictures, and hiked back down.

Once the pavement ended, the rocks and sand started. Some stones were medium-sized (the size of a honey-dew), and others were smaller (the size of a tennis ball).

The rocks hurt my feet because they were so uneven, and several rocks were jagged. The sand was scattered through the trail. It was also pretty dusty.

After three and a half miles, I arrived at Nevada Fall. At the top of the waterfall, there were large flat rocks.

Several tourists were lying around, sunbathing, journaling, and just hanging out.

There was a warning sign that read, "Stay out of the water! Powerful, hidden currents will carry you over the fall. Stay back from the slippery rock at the water's edge. If you go over the fall, you will die." The sign was very blunt, but I don't blame them. It seemed every year there was a story on the news about how someone died because they stood in the water to get a picture, slipped, and were carried over the edge.

It's a large, beautiful waterfall. I could see it a mile away as I was climbing up, and it's a force of nature. I stood on the bridge taking some pictures with the tourists. The sun was warm, and I could feel it soaking into my skin. I sat on the flat rocks and enjoyed the sun for a bit. It was pretty hot, and I was sweating a lot. I decided to eat a snack while taking a break. After about 30 minutes or so, I started again.

Shortly after I continued on the trail, I ran into a couple who stopped me. I was wearing a shirt that said "LA Leggers." The LA Leggers is a running group that meets in Santa Monica every Saturday morning to train for the LA marathon. The season is about seven months long and slowly helps you increase mileage, so you're prepared for a full marathon. They also have half marathon training available, which is what I did. I ran with the group for the last seven years on and off.

I took off my headphones, and the couple said, "Hey! We're Leggers too!" I told them I was hiking the JMT, and they said, "We'll take your picture for you so you can post it for the 'cross-training competition.'"

I didn't realize it, but a photo contest encouraged people to incorporate more cross-training during the week. The funny thing is that when I returned home after the JMT and went for a run, I could barely run. My feet got accustomed to my hiking shoes and the weight of my pack, and my muscles had changed entirely. It took several weeks to work my way back up to running even three to four miles comfortably.

I was happy to run into the couple. They were encouraging and supportive. I continued, and the trail finally leveled out a bit. I knew I was close to the backpackers' campground.

The trail turned to full-on sand. It's tough to hike with a 50-pound pack through the sand. The sun was beating on me, and the sand seemed never-ending.

Around 2:00 pm, I arrived at the backpackers' campground. Three wooden outhouses were up a flight of stairs and only had a toilet in each room.

I walked around the campsites, unsure of where to set up my tent. There weren't many people around. I saw a few tents set up but didn't see anybody at the sites. The campsites had massive tree logs laid down, dividing them. Each one could fit one to two tents.

They had bear lockers at each site too, which was nice. The bear lockers were about four feet wide and 18″ tall. They have a latch, so you can put your food in there and close the latch. Bears can't open it, so they usually don't even try. The ground was all dirt with some twigs. There were so many pine trees; they created a lot of shade. Tree stumps were also everywhere, which made for great chairs.

I picked a site and started to set up my tent. It all felt

bizarre. I didn't know where the people were that had tents set up. Were they inside the tents? Were they hiking a local trail? Why weren't there any people around and why so few tents? It was so quiet.

At least it gave me time to figure out my tent set up without embarrassment. It took me a while because it was a little windy, and I had to keep moving the tent. I wondered, *What was the advice? Set up the tent going with the wind?*

Bees were circling the whole time, and I kept trying to shoo them away.

Looking at the map, I saw there should be a river nearby for water. I walked through the campground and came across a middle-aged couple. They were hanging up some clothes to dry and helped direct me to the river.

When I got to the river, I noticed a little bank to get close to the water. The river was slow, and the section by the bank was still. There were also probably 20 bees checking out the water and sand. I needed water, so I carefully scooped it up in my four-liter bag.

I hooked the bag with dirty water to the clean water bag and tried to hold the dirty water up so gravity would pull the water down into the filter and then into the clean bag. I carefully stayed at the bank for a little while, trying to avoid the bees. I thought, *If I have to use my epi-pen on day one, this will not be good.*

Because I'm paranoid of theft, I brought my backpack with me. I left my food in the bear locker, but I took the rest. I'm used to living in Los Angeles, where you can't just leave things around.

After I filtered the four liters into the clean bag, I scooped up four more liters so I'd have eight liters total. I carried it back to my tent, and there was a good tree there to hang the bag on so it could continue to filter.

The bees were circling all around; regular bees, bumblebees, and wasps. The buzzing sound was terrible. They'd fly right by my ear, which made me swat and start walking in circles to get them away from me.

It was around 4:00 pm, and I wanted to take a nap, but there was a wasp in my tent. I tried multiple techniques to get the wasp out to no avail.

There were now two guys at a nearby campsite. They were sitting on some tree stumps, so I looked over and asked, "Do you know how to get a wasp out of a tent?" They sounded like they were from Germany, looked at me confused, and then said they did not know. I turned back towards my tent and thought, *So much for backpacker comradery.*

The doors on my tent were open, and I had to shake the tent around, trying to get the wasp out. It finally left! I got inside my tent and tried to take a nap.

I still had cell reception, so I was texting friends and family about my journey so far. It was good to lay down, but I couldn't sleep. It was also pretty warm.

I suddenly felt very sad and alone. Maybe it was boredom or not getting any help from the fellow back-packers, but I had an incredible sadness that suddenly sank in. I started to cry quietly. I wondered how I would survive three weeks like this. Did I make a mistake try-ing to hike this alone?

Then I realized a coworker, Tori, had mentioned a few weeks earlier that she could hike in some goodies to me if I wanted. But she'd have to hike in on the week-end because of work. I messaged her, and she was totally game to hike in to see me and bring snacks. I thought it was so nice since we didn't know each other that well.

I looked at my map to try and figure out a trail she could hike in on. It's tough to figure out where you'll be that far in advance. She would drive the four hours to Lone Pine or Independence Friday night and camp to start hiking early Saturday morning.

I knew I had reservations at Muir Trail Ranch on September 11–12th, and she would be on the trail on the 17th. Leaving the ranch on the 12th, I'd be at mile 105. I saw a trail called Taboose Pass Trail. It's at mile 158, so that gave me five days to go 53 miles.

I planned on increasing my pace the second half of the trail, but the only trails she could hike in were Taboose at mile 158 or Kearsarge Pass at mile 180. I wasn't confident I could reach her at mile 180 by the 17th, which would mean I would have to hike 75 miles in five days. We agreed on Taboose Pass, and I said I'd have email access at Muir Trail Ranch in 11 days, so we decided to connect then.

Around 6:00 pm, I started to cook my Pad Thai dinner in my Jetboil. The Jetboil was so great because it protected the flame from wind, and it boiled water at a rapid speed. I was pleased to have eight liters of water so I didn't have to go back to the river.

There was one wasp that buzzed all around my tent while I tried to nap, while I cooked dinner, while I ate dinner, and while I cleaned up. I put on additional bug spray, but it didn't matter. He was not leaving. He would come right up to my face.

I sat on the bear locker and ate but every time the bees buzzed by my ear; I would jump up and walk around in a small circle in my campsite. I must have looked like a crazy person.

Around 7:15 pm, it started to get dark, so I went to the outhouses. I was glad to have my Purell since there was no water to wash up. I got inside my tent and started to journal.

I looked out the tent and could see stars through the giant pine trees. I liked my tent, but I had to open the rain flap to see the stars, and then I felt too exposed. People would be able to see me in the morning.

I gazed at the stars and trees and felt at peace. Once I finished staring, I zipped up the rain flap and went to sleep.

➤ Camped at 6,118 feet
➤ Hiked five miles
➤ 2,600 feet elevation gain

Day

2

Out of Water

I woke up when the sun started to come up around 6:30 am, but the trees were blocking the light. I could hear people cleaning up their campsites, but I was still tired, so I went back to sleep. Around 8:00 am, I got up. I slept in my shorts and shirt from the previous day because it was relatively warm, and my sleeping bag was a 10-degree bag. I didn't want to sleep in my thermals since they're pretty warm. I changed my clothes to my second set of shorts and a T-shirt. Here is the list of clothes I brought:

- Two pair of spandex shorts (black)
- Two technical T-shirts, polyester (one red and one bright green)
- Two long sports bras
- One pair of pants, also rain resistant
- One long sleeve shirt, polyester (light purple)
- Three pairs of underwear (two Ex-Officio and one prAna)
- Two pair of wool hiking socks

- One rain jacket (light gray)
- One down jacket (bright blue)
- One headband that also covers the ears

I know this is an odd mixture. But I choose these clothes based on weight, the ability to wick away sweat, keep me warm, and what was on sale (or I already had). I changed into my red shirt and black spandex shorts. I put my glasses and sandals on and headed to the outhouse.

I walked back to my campsite and made breakfast: freeze-dried scrambled eggs with bacon bits. I was glad I had extra water from my filter, so I didn't have to go back to the river. I also made a latte. Starbucks sells these packets of lattes that have coffee, sugar, and cream. You just have to add hot water. They're delicious.

The packets are bigger than I'd like because they have some air inside. But these delightful lattes were the highlight of my mornings and definitely worth bringing. I had vanilla and white chocolate and each morning looked forward to choosing one. I brought a little blue plastic cup that folded inside itself. Other than that cup and my Jetboil, my only other dish was a hard plastic spork.

I enjoyed my eggs and latte but had to fight with the bees again. I realized they were just curious and looking for food and water. I let them crawl on me and my stuff since swatting them away was useless. I looked around and noticed almost everyone was gone.

There weren't many people at the campsites to begin with, but it looked like the few packed up early and left.

After eating breakfast, I had to clean my Jetboil and cup. I used a little washcloth that is designed for quick drying. I just used my clean water and the washcloth and rinsed them out. It seemed to work just fine. I didn't use soap because even though it was biodegradable, it felt crappy to leave soap suds behind at the campsite.

Packing up my stuff seemed to take an eternity. I had to put my contacts in, put sunblock on, pull my hair back in a ponytail, squeeze my sleeping bag into a compression sack, deflate and roll up my sleeping pad, take my tent down and stuff it into the bag, and get everything back in my backpack. By the time I finished all of this, it was around 11:00 am.

I stopped by the outhouses again on my way out. They were nice to have, but they were very basic.

Getting my backpack on was always a challenge. It was 50 pounds with full food and water. Thankfully, the guy who helped me pick out my pack at REI showed me a technique.

I would put one leg out in front and bend it at a 90-degree angle. I set the backpack on my foot, with the straps hitting my leg. Then, I would pull the pack up to rest on my bent knee. Next, I would put my right arm through the strap. Once that was through, I would swing the backpack around and put my left arm through.

It was super helpful because otherwise, I would not have been able to get that pack on. My rolled-up foam sleeping pad (that I put under my blow-up pad) was rolled up and attached to the outside of my pack at the bottom. My sandals hung from loops at the bottom, one on each side of the foam roll.

I set out a little embarrassed that I was starting so late in the day. But then I told myself, "Hike your own hike." Hiking isn't a competition, and there isn't a "right way to do it."

Yes, there are certain things you need to be prepared for. But I was consciously making an effort to do MY own thing—the way I wanted to do it. No more people-pleasing.

Leaving the campground, the trail was pretty flat with lots of sand and medium-sized rocks. I was surprised by the amount of sand. But once the trail started to climb, it became dirt and medium to large rocks.

It was a lot of climbing. I passed several day-hikers, and they seemed to be running on the trail. I justified my slower pace because their packs were so much smaller and lighter. Once I passed the trail entry to Half Dome a mile and half in, the people disappeared.

The terrain changed frequently. It was rocky, lots of trees, and would randomly go into a dark forest for about ten minutes. The first time I entered into more of a forest, I was listening to my music, looking down at the trail, and suddenly almost ran into a deer.

I looked up, and he was on the path about 15 feet in front of me. I stopped and turned off my music. He froze, and we both stood there, still, staring at each other. He was huge and beautiful with curious eyes. There wasn't anybody around, and looking into his eyes, it felt like we could communicate. Then he slowly continued into the forest. In the distance, I could see him meet up with a couple of other deer.

I came to the top of a ridge, and looking out to the

right, I could see substantial sweeping mountains. There weren't as many trees, and the ones that were there were cut in half and were burnt. I wasn't sure if it was because of a beetle that had been killing trees or a fire.

The view was terrific, and it felt good that I had climbed up there to earn it. I took a picture and posted it on Facebook. I still had service up there, so I figured, why not? About two hours later, I no longer had any cell service. It wouldn't return for several days.

I continued on the trail, which was pretty well maintained. There were giant tree trunks that had been cut because they had fallen on the trail. Sometimes I'd walk right through the tree since an opening inside of it was made to make room. Other times, I'd see pieces of the tree trunk that had been cut, scattered around.

Then I went through a section that looked super creepy; nothing but tree trunks around, 10–20 feet high, all black. It looked like a fire had ravaged the place. It was sweltering, and I was sweating profusely.

Many of the small creeks that I passed were dry. California was currently in the worst drought it has ever experienced, and I started to worry that I'd run out of water.

I came to a tiny creek and noticed a man and woman drinking from it. They had a straw filter they were using and had to get right up to the water and suck through the straw. I didn't see them until I was already crossing, and we just nodded.

Shortly after passing that couple, a guy coming from the other direction warned me to get water at the next creek. He said it was small and kind of brownish, but all of the other streams were dry. About half an hour later, I arrived at the creek, and it was only slightly bigger than the one that the couple was drinking from. I figured I better stop and get water since I was almost out. It was also a good time to eat lunch.

This little creek was in a section that was a dense forest. It was dark because of the tree cover and a lot cooler. I noticed a giant rock at the bank of the river crossing, so I set my backpack near there and used the rock as my chair. I could only fill my water filter bag about halfway because the water was so shallow and wasn't flowing very fast. I put the bag of dirty water on top of the rock and the clean bag on the ground to let gravity do its job.

I pulled out my little triangles of soft cheese, rice crackers (that were mostly broken), and beef jerky. As I started to eat, the couple I had passed earlier walked up. Their names were Mark and Annie.

They asked if I had a water filter, and I showed it to them. The couple looked exhausted and said they only had those straw filters. Their hydration bladders were out of water, and they couldn't refill them without a filter. I told them I'd fill their bladders, no problem. I gave them the one to two liters that were already filtered, and then I scooped up more water to be filtered. We chatted while I ate lunch and the water was filtering.

It turns out Mark and Annie were on a week-long trip hiking and backpacking through Yosemite to celebrate Annie completing her Ph.D. in psychology. I congratulated Annie on completing her degree, and she said, "Yeah, but I already have a job and won't get a raise." I said, "Maybe it will pay off at your next job."

Advanced degrees are interesting. The company I worked for would pay 100% of tuition and books for any accredited school. I had worked there for nine years and never went to get my Master's degree. I struggled to figure out what I would major in. I majored in Broadcasting and Film for my undergraduate degree and struggled even then to narrow it down. I didn't want to get an MBA just to get one. I wanted to study what I am passionate about but could never quite narrow it down. My lack of decision meant I had gone nine years without taking advantage of a great program. As my Critical Thinking college professor once told me, "Not to decide is to decide."

Mark and Annie lived in San Francisco and hadn't done a lot of backpacking. They were embarrassed that they didn't think about how they'd refill their hydration bladders. They also didn't realize they'd go through so much water, but it was hot out. I filled up their hydration bladders, and they said they would thank me with some whiskey at Sunrise High Sierra Camp.

We were both headed there to camp that night. I originally planned on hiking farther than Sunrise High Sierra Camp, but with the elevation gain and an almost full pack, it wasn't happening. Mark and Annie were friendly, and it made me feel better about "trail friends." They joked that I'd catch up to them in no time since I had passed them earlier.

They took off, and I finished my lunch. I enjoyed some peanut butter too. I continue to climb, and the steep terrain made it challenging. About an hour later, I came across Mark and Annie, along with several guys, at a small creek. Mark and Annie had just added more water to their packs and were taking off. They all warned me that Sunrise High Sierra camp ran out of water and I should carry extra water.

One of the guys was from Dallas, Texas, and said, "This is the last water until Cathedral Lakes (about six miles away). Sunrise is all out of water." I said, "Seriously? I was going to stay there. I just filled up my water and don't want to get my filter out again." In his southern accent, he said, "My rule is never pass up water." So I decided to get my filter out.

That backpackers' campground is on a mountainside, and the lake is on the other side of the mountain. The water is pumped in from the lake for backpackers. However, the lake mostly ran dry, and a ranger had just shut off the water pipe. I didn't know any of this, so I was grateful for the information. However, I was annoyed that I needed to take off my backpack and get my filter out again.

While I filtered the water, I chatted with the group of guys. The guy from Texas said, "Crazy! That couple (Mark and Annie)—I used to sit behind her family at church in Texas. What a small world!" They hadn't known each other before. He was almost finished hiking the JMT, going northbound. He said, "It's been great! But man, my butt is like a racetrack! I need a lot of Vaseline." It's fascinating how strangers open up when you're in the middle of nowhere.

The guy from Texas and his group passed Sunrise High Sierra Camp because of the lack of water and planned to camp wherever they could find a flat spot.

I filled my hydration bladder, my 1-liter bottle, my 12-ounce shaker bottle (for protein shakes) and filtered about two liters to my clean water bag. I carried more water than most people because I drink a lot and sweat a lot. Now, I had to haul even more.

I attached the clean bag of water to the outside of my backpack because it wouldn't fit inside my pack unless it was empty. It swung side to side as I climbed and sometimes hit the back of my arm. My pack felt so heavy because the last two miles to camp were all climbing. I had to keep pausing for 20 seconds or so to catch my breath.

Dusk started setting in because it was around 6:30 pm, and the sun was setting behind the mountain. I felt like I would fall over from exhaustion.

As I reached the top, it flattened to this beautiful yellow meadow. The sun was slowly creeping behind the mountain, and I was getting nervous. I didn't see any campground, and my GPS watch said I had already completed the mileage needed to get to the camp.

Then I saw a little wooden sign that said "Backpackers' Campground." I was confused because I didn't see anything other than the sign. There was a little trail that went off the JMT into the side of the mountain. I followed the path and, after about five minutes, saw there were little flat spots that made up the campground.

I saw a small pen with donkeys to the left and a bonfire going with a small group of people to the right. I climbed up the mountain, unsure of where to go.

I was dirty, smelly, sweaty, and exhausted. I saw a guy walking close to me with sandals and a coffee cup in his hand. I asked desperately, "Where do I go?" My baseball hat was blocking my vision because he was slightly higher up on a rock. I had my headphones in my ears, but the music was turned off.

I took off my sunglasses, looked up at him, and realized he was very attractive. He was around my age and had slightly wavy dark brown hair about chin length pulled back. He smiled beautifully and said, "I'll show you around! I'm just out for my evening stroll." I quickly became aware of how dirty and smelly I was.

His name was Justin. He showed me the two wooden outhouses that were hidden. There were also bear boxes to put food. The campsites were spread out and literally on the side of a mountain cliff. We climbed all around as Justin pointed out, "See that flat spot, that's a site."

Most flat spots were only big enough to hold a 1–2 person tent. Some had tree trunks for a chair. Justin warned me that the water was shut off. He said he was filling his water bottle when the ranger shut it off, saying the lake was dry. I said, "Yeah, I was warned coming up here, so I carried extra water. I actually carried about five liters up here."

Justin also warned me that it was freezing the night before. We were at 9,000 feet, so it was much higher than my previous night, at 6,000 feet.

Justin said, "Let me show you where my tent is." We continued to climb, and his tent was on the very top spot, on top of a rock. He said he wanted to avoid the trees that would block the sun in the morning and pointed to where the sun would rise. Then he pointed to the left of his tent and said, "There's a spot there." We walked over, and just past it was an old den area for donkeys. It didn't look like it was used any longer.

I didn't want Justin to think I was creepy, staying right next to him, so I walked back down to other spots. There were people here and there, but I didn't see Mark and Annie, so no whiskey for me. I wanted to bond with hikers, drinking whiskey.

I decided to go back up next to Justin. There was something comforting about him. He was friendly, and it felt nice to have someone nearby. Plus, I wanted the sun to hit my tent in the morning too. When I got back up there, Justin said, "Hey, you're back!" That made me feel special.

I started to set up my tent, sleeping pad, and sleeping bag. I cooked my dinner, another freeze-dried meal (chicken and rice), and took out my contacts before it was too dark.

My tent was on the side of the cliff on a rock bed, so I had a hard time getting my stakes in the ground. I thought, *If I roll over too much, I could roll right off this cliff!*

I sat on a large rock next to my tent (level with my tent, overlooking the meadow) and ate my dinner from my Jetboil. It was almost dark out. While I was cooking dinner, Justin was standing by his tent, taking pictures of the meadow with a large, professional camera. By the time I was eating dinner, he was in his tent. I sat on the rock, looking at the meadow.

About 50 feet below my tent was a pen for donkeys, and there were about four donkeys inside. There are donkeys on the trail that will carry supplies for hikers. Hikers carry the water and supplies they need for the day, but a guide ties the donkeys together, and they carry all of the other supplies. The guide will ride the lead donkey. That way, hikers only have to carry a day pack.

I thought, *That's not fair. That's not real backpacking.* But then I had to remind myself, *Hike your own hike.* It might not be my style of backpacking, but it's okay that other people choose that.

Justin was right about the cold. I put my pants on over my shorts to eat dinner. I also put my jacket on. It was hard to eat dinner because I didn't have much of an appetite. The small group of people at the bottom had a fire going. I wished I could have had a fire. But there wasn't a fire pit nearby, and with the drought and California fires, I didn't even want to bother. Their voices echoed up the mountain, and they seemed to be having a good time.

After dinner, I grabbed my headlight and climbed down to the outhouses. I realized I hadn't used the restroom since the outhouses at my last campground. I knew it was hot, but it made me realize I must have been sweating out a lot of my water.

I struggled to find my way to the outhouse and back again because there wasn't a trail to my spot. I ended up walking right by other tents and had to apologize for being on their site. I got back to my tent and laid on the rock, staring at the stars.

After about five minutes, I got into my tent and put on my thermals. They were skin-tight, designed that way to keep your body heat in. It got cold very quickly. I had a hard time sleeping because I kept hearing my ground cover under my tent crinkle due to the wind. At least I hoped it was wind and not critters.

Then I heard animal noises. I kept reminding myself, *It's just the donkeys, they're not far away. It's not bears.* I was terrified that a bear would get me. I put my food in the bear box by the outhouses, but I used my washcloth to rinse out my Jetboil and hung the washcloth from a tree nearby. I was scared a bear would smell food particles on the cloth. It's crazy how the mind wanders and starts imagining every worst possible outcome. It was a long, cold night.

➤ Camped at 9,333 feet
➤ Hiked 8.5 miles

Day

3

Generous Gestures

I woke up around 6:00 am when the sun came shining on my tent, but I laid in bed until a little after 7:00 am. I changed my clothes, got out of my tent, and felt the crisp air. I was delighted to have that sun hit me in the morning because it was still pretty cold.

I made oatmeal and added raisins and brown sugar. I also made my delicious latte. As I was eating my oatmeal, I noticed my friendly neighbor, Justin, awake and hanging out by his tent. I walked closer to him while eating my oatmeal from my Jetboil. He was above me on the large rock where his tent sat.

I said, "You weren't kidding about the cold. Dang! It was so cold and windy last night!" He agreed and said he slept in his coat and hat. He also mentioned that he thinks chipmunks were trying to get into his tent because he kept hearing little rustlings around, making it hard to sleep. It made me feel better that I wasn't the only one who was a little creeped out about the little sounds.

Our campsites overlooked a peaceful yellow meadow, and there was a hazy dew cloud hovering over it. Justin said he got some great pictures when he woke up.

Justin was an experienced backpacker, but he was struggling to find the right place for his bear canister. They were required in the park, but he wasn't used to them. Justin put his can on the outside of the backpack, but the next day, he moved it inside, hoping it wouldn't be such a nuisance.

Justin and I chatted, and I got to know him a little. He grew up on the east side of Pennsylvania, lived in Colorado for a little while, and now lived in Portland, Oregon. He had moved to Portland for grad school and stayed. He was a software engineer and was able to get a month off work (unpaid) to do some traveling. He planned to spend around four days in Yosemite backpacking on various trails.

After Yosemite, Justin planned on going to Glacier

National Park in Montana, Utah, and then to Colorado to visit friends. As we were chatting, he pointed to my campsite and said, "A chipmunk is on your bear canister."

I looked over and tried to get there quickly to close my canister. As I approached, the chipmunk jumped up to the large rock next to my bear can and knocked my latte over! I scrambled over the rocks and was left with just a little bit of coffee in the cup. I must have looked like a cartoon character chasing this rodent. It was highly embarrassing.

I asked Justin where his breakfast was, and he said, "I ran out of water. Did you say you carried up five liters?" I laughed and asked if he needed some. He explained that he just wanted to make his tea. I gave Justin about half a liter to make his tea and so that he'd have some water to get him over the hill to the lake where he could filter more water.

Justin and I continued to chat while we both packed up our campsites. He was really friendly, and I enjoyed our conversation. He told me that he rents part of his house out on Airbnb because it has a separate area for living, like a duplex. He said he had a couple of girls from New York stay there one time, and they complained about having ants. He said, "They probably live in a high rise in New York and have never seen an ant. Well, it's called nature."

Of course, I took longer to pack up because I just couldn't figure out a faster way to get everything done. I was close to being all packed up, and he was ready to go.

Justin came down to my campsite, and we continued to chat while I finished up. We talked about gear, and he asked if he could handle some of the stuff, like my tent. He wanted to see if it really was lightweight. I had told him about how I had a friend who promoted lightweight backpacking, so I was trying the best I could.

When I was trying to fill the top part of my back-pack (the lid), lots of little stuff in stuff-sacs started to fall out, and I had to grab them. Of course, it was my lotion, sunblock, journal, glasses, things like that. Justin laughed and said, "A lightweight backpacker would have a field day with all that stuff you're carrying!" Embarrassed yet again, I smiled and said, "It's fine. I can carry it."

Before we headed out, we walked down to the two outhouses. Once we were finished, we both started put-ting on our backpacks. I needed to take the trail down to hit the JMT again, and he had to continue up the moun-tain to get on the other side. There was a couple nearby who were going to use the outhouses, and they said hello.

I really wanted to stay in touch with Justin and didn't know how to say goodbye and get his information, and now there were people nearby. We high-fived, and he said, "Find me on Facebook." He told me his last name, which was unique. He spelled it, and I repeated it out loud. In my head, I thought, *As soon as I stop for water, I'm taking out my journal and writing it down so I don't forget.*

Justin said, "Oh, you'll never remember it!" Then he found a business card he had in the side pocket of his backpack. He handed it to me, and it made me happy because he actually wanted to stay in touch. He wasn't just saying it. He made my first night away from the val-ley much easier. Do you ever meet someone and instantly feel connected? That's what I felt about him. We said goodbye and headed in different directions.

Once I got back on the JMT, the trail was relatively flat, but it was quickly warming up. I was sweating a lot, and it was four miles until the next water source. The last water I had come across was about two and a half miles before I arrived at Sunrise High Sierra Camp, and I used that water for the climb up, dinner, breakfast, to clean up a bit, and gave some to Justin.

I ran out of water about two miles into my hike that morning. The sun was beating, and there wasn't any shade. It's funny how much you think about water when you're in the sun, sweating, have a dry mouth, and there is no water in sight. All of the streams I passed were dry.

About four miles into my hike, I could see Upper Cathedral Lake. I took the small trail to the lake and couldn't wait to drink that water. There were two guys

about 50 feet away on a large flat rock getting some water. I stopped at the first part of the lake, where there was a small section of rock I could balance on and scoop up water. I tried to use a nearby tree to filter my water and use gravity, but there weren't many trees. The trees around were all tiny and wouldn't support the water. I finally found one that worked. I drank some water as soon as it was filtered. I filled up my hydration pack and bottles and had a protein shake. This all took about 45 minutes.

I continued on the trail, and it went up and down several times. At least several parts of the trail had shade. There was a train of four donkeys that came through with supplies, so I moved for them to pass. Then I came across a sign that read "trail restoration" for a section of the JMT. There was an alternative route, and it added about a mile and a half.

There were a fair number of day hikers in that section. They either didn't have a backpack, or they had a tiny one. They seemed so fresh. I could even smell their soap and shampoo.

The pocketbook map I had said there was no camping within four miles of Tuolumne Meadows. When I picked up my permit, I thought the ranger said there was no camping four miles before and four miles after Tuolumne Meadows. If that were true, it would mean I'd hike six miles for the day if I stopped before Tuolumne Meadows or 14 miles if I stopped after.

Tuolumne Meadows is a popular place for tourists, and there is car camping there. You must have a permit to camp there, and it's hard to get. When I left Sunrise

High Sierra Camp in the morning, I thought I could hike the 14 miles. However, with stopping for water, the heat, the added mile and a half, I was feeling tired.

I stopped for lunch on a rock that was right off the trail. I ate some tuna, peanut butter, and beef jerky. A few day-hikers passed, and it made me feel embarrassed. I wanted to say, "I'm hiking the whole JMT, and this is my third day." As if I needed to explain why I was so tired, dirty, and sweaty.

I continued, and I felt like I should have already made it to Tuolumne Meadows, and my watch also indicated I already passed it based on mileage. I thought there could be no way I missed it. It was supposed to be a popular spot, with a café and everything. I felt like I couldn't hike four miles beyond Tuolumne Meadows because it was getting late, and I was so exhausted. Each mile was taking me about 30 minutes because of the terrain and my heavy backpack. I desperately wanted to see if there was an opening at the lodge and I could get a room.

It was getting later, and I was in a very green area with lots of trees and tall grass. I came across a guy in his 40–50's, and I asked him where Tuolumne Meadows was. He said, "You passed it. The lodge is just up here, but you have to go off-trail a little."

I was devastated. I said, "But I thought the trail went through Tuolumne Meadows, and there was a grill. I can't hike another four miles to camp. I've already hiked 11½ miles, and I'm exhausted."

He said, "There was a backpackers' camp in between the car camping spots, and that's where the grill was." I was confused and said, "I thought I wasn't allowed to stay at Tuolumne Meadows?" I figured I'd give it a try because I felt like I couldn't go any farther. The man said his car was parked near the backpackers' campground, so he'd take me there. I was thankful for his help because the forest was dense, and clearly, I missed it already.

I ended up backtracking about a mile and a half. The man and I both got a little confused and had to ask a few people where the backpackers' campground was. The car camping was spread out in the trees, and it felt like a maze in a forest. The man told me he had cell service, but I did not. We tried to use GPS to help us navigate, but it didn't work. I was disappointed about my lack of cell service because I wanted to call the lodge to see if there was an available room. Exhaustion will make you feel pretty desperate.

I knew the rooms were booked far in advance, but I was hoping for a cancelation. The lodge wasn't on the JMT, and it would require more walking, so I wasn't going to try to find it if I wasn't sure they had a room.

We were almost to the backpackers' campground, and the man left to find his car. I eventually found the camp and saw a sign that read "walk-in backpackers." I went up a slight hill, and it said as long as you had a wilderness permit, which I had, it was $6 per person per night.

It's funny; before this hike, I had no idea that backpackers' campgrounds existed or what they were like. I only car camped, and that was years ago, growing up. Backpackers' campgrounds are very basic and just provide some small flat spots to put a very small tent. This one had a few picnic tables and fire pits, which was nice.

As I walked into the campground area, I saw a tall, thin guy around 25 years old with long hair pulled back walking towards me. His name was Tom. I asked him, "Where do I go?"

He was really friendly and explained what I needed to do. He said a ranger told him that each spot is designed to hold a few tents. He showed me his tent, which wasn't far away. There was an open spot near him, and he said two guys paid for a site but left and said they might come back. But it was 6:00 pm, and they hadn't come back. They left their receipt under a rock.

I decided Tom seemed nice and cool, so I would take the spot nearby. However, another tent with two guys in their 20's was set up near our area. They were a bit farther back but in between Tom and me. I had a picnic table next to my tent, and so did the guys. I didn't know if the people who paid for that site would come back, and you had to put a receipt on your tent. I only had $20 bills, and the fee was $6, and it had to be dropped into a box.

I asked the annoying guys next to me if they had change for a $20 bill. They said no, but Tom overheard me and said, "Are you just trying to pay the fee?" I said yes, and he gave me the $6, so I didn't have to put a $20 bill in. He left and headed to the store nearby because they had firewood.

After I set up my tent, I walked down to the restroom to wash some clothes. The bathroom had four stalls, one sink for washing hands/face, and one sink for washing clothes or dishes. I changed my clothes and put on my pants and long sleeve shirt since they were clean and it was starting to get cold. I tried to wash up a bit using a small washcloth I had, but it was pretty tricky to do in a bathroom stall. I wiped my arms and legs down and felt a little better that I got the dust off.

The sun started to go down around 7:00 pm and was dark by 7:30 pm because the mountains blocked the sun. As I washed the two outfits that I'd worn the last couple of days, it got dark. I realized there was not a light in the bathroom, so I had to use my headlamp. The water was freezing, but it was drinkable, so I could fill up my water bottles.

A few other people were coming in to rinse dishes, but they had to wait for me to finish washing my clothes. I used my little bottle of Dr. Bronner's soap, but it didn't work too well. I couldn't plug the drain in the sink, and there aren't many suds with this soap, so I went through a lot of soap.

In true Christy-style, I went to reach for the small two-ounce bottle to add more soap and knocked it off the sink's ledge. The bottle had a screw-on top, and that also had a flip to it, so you could just flip the top open, and a small hole would allow soap to come out at a reasonable pace. Somehow when it fell to the floor, the lid came off completely, and half of the bottle emptied before I could pick it up and stop the flow. Nothing is easy when you're backpacking.

As I washed my clothes and the sun was starting to set, a woman around 40–45 years old came in to wash her face in the other sink. We started talking, and she said, "Wow! You're doing this by yourself? There are four of us in our group. We're from Washington D.C., and we were supposed to hike from Tuolumne Meadows to Red's Meadow (40 miles), but after hiking today, we turned around and came back to the campground. We're taking a bus tomorrow to San Francisco to explore for a few days. Maybe we'll do a bike tour. But we realized we're too out of shape for this trail. We'll explore San Francisco until we have to go back to D.C."

I couldn't believe they didn't even make it one day. They had camped in the backpackers' campground the night before and were supposed to be on the trail. But in one day, they realized they had not trained properly for the amount of climbing and wouldn't be able to continue hiking, so they turned back. And this was a relatively more manageable part of the trail.

The woman also told me she met a couple who started in Tuolumne Meadows, but once they got to Donahue Pass (the first major mountain pass 12 miles away), they had difficulty breathing and had to turn back. They were also staying the night at the campground and planned on taking the bus out of Yosemite.

These stories made me feel good because I had prepared for the physical nature of the trail. Even though I could stand to lose some weight, I was in better shape than these people. It also made me feel a little nervous about what laid ahead. If people were turning back that quickly, what was so bad about the upcoming sections?

There was also a part of me that felt irritated. I mean, permits are extremely difficult to get, and people worldwide want to hike this trail. It felt disappointing that people would get their permits and not spend the next six months properly preparing. Those permits could have gone to someone who had prepared and wanted to hike it but didn't get a permit.

While I was in the restroom, I took out my contacts and brushed my teeth, using my headlamp. When I got back to my campsite, I strung a rope across two big trees to line-dry my clothes. I had to do this in the dark, which was fine because it's a little embarrassing to hang out underwear for the world to see.

I had to make my dinner in the dark, but at least I had a picnic table. I used my headlamp and boiled another freeze-dried dinner. While I ate my dinner, I could hear the two guys near me chatting. They were stereotypical "dudes" and it was annoying to listen to their conversation. They were in their tent, but they weren't far away. Tents might give the appearance of privacy, but they do not give you sound privacy.

At one point, I heard, "You mean you both have the same laptop . . . what's the deal with her?!" I thought, *That's what guys talk about when they talk about girls? Laptops? Why does that matter?*

After I cleaned up from dinner, I saw Tom come out of his tent and start gathering twigs nearby. He had a fire pit by his tent with a table that he moved to the fire. I walked over to him (about 25 feet away from my tent) and helped him gather twigs. He said the wood was too expensive, so he was collecting what he could find. We grabbed little broken twigs and dead pine cones. We sat by the tiny fire and talked. Every five minutes or so, the fire would start to die out, and we had to look for more things to burn. Tom had a little bottle of whiskey, and I was a little sad he didn't offer me any.

Tom was also hiking the whole JMT and was planning on finishing at the end of September (taking about four weeks). He said he'd done a fair amount of hiking and backpacking but was not used to such a large backpack. His pack was about 50–55 pounds, and the trail was tough with a pack that heavy, especially with the elevation.

Tom took out some food earlier that evening and threw it away. You see, even when you want to lighten your load, there is no trash can available, so you have to keep carrying it. But there were large, metal, locked trash bins in the campground (primarily for car campers), so he was finally able to let go of some stuff. It made me feel good to know an experienced hiker also found the trail challenging, and the number of items required to carry for that long was more than he was used to. My 50-pound pack didn't seem so heavy after all.

Tom grew up in a small mountain town near Denver and Vail. He moved to Florida for two years because he worked for a company that made soap and similar items. It was a small company, but they grew and started to produce more products and were moving the plant to Florida. Tom started working there because of his girlfriend (she worked there too). The company wanted him to run the production in Florida, so he and his girlfriend moved there for the opportunity.

Tom and I laughed about how we both dislike Florida. I mean, it's hot and super humid, and all the crazy news stories originate in Florida. Tom said he and his girlfriend broke up a couple of months ago. He quit his job, got rid of his apartment, and hiked a bit in Virginia on the Appalachian Trail. He was approved for the Frontier Airlines credit card, and part of the promotion was that he received enough points for a plane ticket. He flew into Fresno and took a bus to Yosemite Valley to start the JMT. He had a return ticket to Virginia at the end of the month but didn't know what he'd do.

Everything Tom owned was in his backpack. He didn't have a smartphone, just a basic phone. He said for the winter, he might do some seasonal work at a ski resort or a volunteer job that covered room and board. He said, "As long as this money takes me." He didn't have much, and I thought it was so sweet that he gave me the $6 without question to help me.

That seems to be how it goes. The people with the least are the most generous. I offered to buy him breakfast the following day at the café. He had a lovely soul, and I could feel his heartache. When he talked about his breakup, I could tell it really affected him.

It made me think about my husband and how relationships can mess you up emotionally. I didn't talk about my separation or mention my husband to Tom. I couldn't bring myself to admit that I was struggling and didn't know what was in my future.

After talking for a while, Tom and I headed to our tents to go to sleep. It was cold, and I journaled for a little bit. I slept okay, but it was clear I was in a backpackers' campground. I could hear people from time to time or see the light from someone walking by. When I set up my tent, I thought I was on a flat spot but I occasionally slid in my tent, falling off my sleeping pad. It made for a restless night.

➤ Camped at 8,646 feet
➤ Hiked 13 miles

Day

4

Wrong Turn

The morning was cold yet again, and the sun couldn't get through the trees. I didn't want to get out of my tent in the cold, but I had to use the restroom. I put on my pants and long sleeve shirt and headed to the toilet. As I headed back from the bathroom, I ran into Tom. He was all packed up and ready to head out.

Tom said, "I'm going to eat at the grill. Maybe I'll see you there." I was bummed because I wasn't even close to being packed up. He said he wasn't trying to do any crazy mileage that day, so he'd probably run into me. I told him that I had reservations at Muir Trail Ranch on September 11th and booked two nights to have a rest day. We said our goodbyes, and I started packing up my campsite.

It was cold and cloudy outside, very different from the last two days, which were sunny and hot. I went to take my clothes off the rope and discovered they were still damp, including my two pairs of socks. It was too cold overnight, and they didn't dry.

I kept my pants, long sleeve shirt, and coat on and packed everything up, except for one pair of shorts, one shirt, one sports bar, and one pair of socks. I tied them to the outside of my pack so they could (hopefully) air dry some more. I didn't cook breakfast, so it was easier to pack up, but it still took much longer than anybody else ever takes.

I headed down to the café, which was just past the car camping section. The café was off of a paved road, and there were lots of people there in regular clothes. I got in line, feeling a little self-conscious because I was smelly, dirty, and not wearing a bra.

It's a strange feeling to be in public without a bra. I had a shirt and a coat on but still felt exposed. I got in line to place an order and saw a delicious breakfast sandwich that looked so good; I had to order it. I also bought some honeydew slices and a coffee.

While I was in line, I chatted with two girls who

were impressed I was doing the whole JMT. I asked them if they could get my small, pink pouch from the lid of my backpack. That backpack was so heavy and so much work to put on; I couldn't imagine taking it off and putting it back on in the tiny café. They were really sweet and got my pouch out for me so I could pay for my breakfast. I was able to snag the last honeydew, which I was pleased about since I hadn't eaten any fresh fruit in days.

I took my breakfast outside to the picnic tables. I took off my backpack and sat down at a table by myself. Nearby, a group of guys in their 20's that sounded like they were from Europe were speaking another language. They seemed to be talking about me and watched me take off my huge pack. Of course, I dropped my camera and looked like an amateur.

There was a line of people waiting for a bus outside in the small parking lot. I ate my breakfast in the cold and cloudy weather, hoping it wouldn't rain.

Once I finished eating, I went to the outdoor restroom. It was an accessible restroom, so it was pretty big, and I changed my clothes. I really dislike hiking in pants and long sleeves because I heat up too much and it feels suffocating. Even though it was cold out, I figured it would warm up again like the past few days. My hope of the clothes drying out while attached to my pack was broken when I touched them—still damp and cold!

I took deep breaths as I put the bra, shirt, and shorts on. It was a cold, clammy feeling. Putting on the socks was the worst part—cold, damp, wool socks. I regretted washing my clothes. I would have preferred dirty socks to cold, wet socks.

As I was heading out, the line of people was heading to the bus. They were all wearing jackets and pants, and here I was, wearing my damp shorts and T-shirt.

I walked through Tuolumne Meadows, and the path was straight-up sand. Lots of sand for about half a mile, which is very hard to hike in. After half a mile, I came to a junction in the tree canopy that had a sign. I stopped to read the sign and to see which path I needed to take.

There was a guy about 23 years old staring at the sign. He was wearing blue shorts, about knee length, and a blue T-shirt. He had a large backpack with an external frame and lots of stuff hanging off of it. He was wearing a baseball hat and had a babyface.

The sign was confusing and didn't say where we were in relation to the map. I introduced myself and found out his name was Justin. He would hike four miles on the JMT and then would need to cut across to another trail. Since we were headed in the same direction, we agreed which path was correct and started hiking together.

The path was pretty steep, but I didn't want to seem like I couldn't keep up, so we hiked pretty quickly. We talked as we hiked, and I was often struggling for breath.

Justin grew up just north of the Lake of the Ozarks in Missouri. He was attending college but was then accepted into an intelligence program for the Navy, so he joined and dropped out of college. He had recently been assigned to a base in Fresno, California.

Justin didn't want to be in California, but since he would be there for the next three years, he figured he'd see as much as he could while he was there. That morning, Justin left Fresno at 3:00 am to drive up to Yosemite.

He wanted to arrive at the permit office at 8:00 am when they opened so he could get a walk-up permit. It was Labor Day weekend, and he had two to three days to hike. They had a permit available for some nearby lakes, so he took it.

Justin's pack was huge with a lot of gear. It was the first backpack that I saw with an external frame. We talked about what equipment we had and the quality (or lack thereof for him). He said, "All of your gear must be at least $600!" I laughed and said, "Well, my sleeping bag alone cost $500." Justin couldn't believe it, and I don't blame him. I could not have afforded all this great equipment when I was in my early 20's. I justified the high price tags as being the cost of a three-week vacation as well as gear that I could reuse.

We talked about gun control and the military. At one point, I got a little nervous, considering I was hiking with a stranger in the woods, with nobody around at all, talking about guns. I thought, *What if he has a gun and he's luring me on this path that we haven't seen anybody on?* Then I reminded myself that I have pretty good intuition, and he seemed fine. But if anybody overheard our conversation, they'd probably be concerned.

After a mile and a half, we came to a river with a massive crossing. There was also a road nearby that we could hear cars on. We both thought it seemed strange and the river didn't seem very crossable there. We pulled out our maps and realized we had made the wrong decision when we were at the junction earlier. The good news was that the trail we were on followed the direction of the JMT, but it looked to be about a mile away. We had climbed up and down a lot of rocks, and neither of us wanted to backtrack.

We decided to cut through the woods, and we'd also have to climb up and down a small mountain to reach the JMT. If we hit the JMT correctly, it would put us on the part of the trail that started to go south (it was previously going east).

Justin and I went off-trail and used his compass to help us navigate through the woods. I felt much better about doing this with a military guy. The ground was definitely not a trail, and many dead trees were lying on the ground that we had to climb over. Some were very large, and Justin helped me. I had a hard time getting my legs over the trees, especially with a large, heavy backpack.

The ground was crunchy with pine cones all around. It was all very dry. At one point, we both got stuck in some thorn bushes. It was quiet and a little scary because it was so dense. It was an adventure, for sure.

Justin had his compass out most of the time so we could follow it, and we joked about how ridiculous we looked, attempting to cross through a dense, dry forest. I asked if I could take his picture, and he agreed. I had regretted not getting a picture of the other guys I met, so I sucked up my embarrassment and asked. I'm happy to have that picture and to remember our adventure.

After about a mile, we came to a river that we had to cross. It wasn't crossable where we were without taking off our shoes, so we walked downstream a bit. We found a section with many rocks exposed, and we thought we could jump from rock to rock and not take off our shoes.

This strategy was how I had crossed all the rivers so far (except for a few with bridges), but this one was by far the widest (about 50–60 feet). The rocks were spread out, so we had to really stretch our legs and use our trekking poles. Justin crossed first and made it, so I followed. I almost fell in at one point and slightly screamed. But I made it!

Justin and I continued to hike along the river on flat rocks and dirt, and it was warming up. The trees were also opening up, and the sun was beating down. We stopped for five minutes under a small tree for some shade to drink some water and eat a snack. I had a power bar and watched a deer drink water nearby.

I could feel a blister on my big left toe, and I thought it was developing because of my wet socks. After about two miles, we made it to the JMT crossing and the path Justin needed to reach his lake. We said our goodbyes and thanked each other for the help making it back to the trail. I wanted to stay in touch somehow but didn't want to seem like a creep, so we just said goodbye.

I continued hiking through Lyell Canyon. I thought about how fun it was to hike with Justin and go off-trail. I also thought it was funny and ironic that so far, the people I met and talked to for a while were named Justin, Tom, and Justin again. It would be hilarious if the next person I met and spoke to was named Tom.

The grass was yellow, dry, and spotty. For the first time, the trail seemed fairly flat. Lyell Canyon was just that, a canyon. To my left was a river, and just above it was a large mountain full of pine trees. Ahead of me were more peaks, jagged in the distance. To my right were more pine trees ascending a mountain.

The trail was very narrow but well-marked. Now that I was getting away from most tourists and day hikers, seeing people became less frequent. My blister was pulsing with each step, and I was in a lot of pain. Then my right foot started to get a blister.

I stopped at a rock that was right off the trail so I could sit down. I figured I should eat lunch too. It was about 3:00 pm. I pulled out my prosciutto slices and a block of cheese. I ate them together while propping my feet up on a small rock across the trail.

As I was eating lunch, a couple came by, Paige and Pablo. We chatted for a bit, and they seemed to be looking at my food. I figured they thought I was eating at a weird time and some fancy meat. Paige and Pablo were in their early 20's and were from San Diego. They were athletic and in good shape. Pablo looked like a hippy with wild hair that was somewhat long. Paige had long brown hair and a great smile.

They were friendly and asked if I was looking for a campsite. I said I would be soon but wasn't sure where to go. The couple continued hiking, and about five minutes later, they yelled down from some rocks and said they found some sites. I told them I might go there.

As I was packing up, a woman named Amy and her husband were passing by. We both had our turquoise bandanas on display (mine hung on my front strap so I could use it to wipe off sweat from my face). The bandana was to show that we were both part of the Facebook group, Ladies of the JMT. The bandana was so that women could recognize and support each other on the trail.

Amy was very excited to meet another Lady of the JMT. I was also pretty thrilled since she was the first one I had seen on the trail. Amy and her husband were doing a section hike of the JMT, not the entire JMT. We talked about the trail, and they were going north-bound. Amy wanted to document our meeting and asked to take a picture. It made me feel so good that I wasn't the only one who wanted pictures of people I met on the trail. Her husband took our picture, and they continued northbound.

I kept hiking southbound and contemplated staying near Paige and Pablo. They seemed really sweet and said they'd be fishing at the river nearby. This would be my first campsite that did not have a bear box or an out-house, and I was a little unsure where I was supposed to set up a tent. Being near them seemed like a good idea.

On the other hand, it was only about 3:30 pm, and I had only hiked about six to seven miles for the day. I planned on making it much farther because the next day, I would be hiking over Donahue pass, the pass that I kept hearing was challenging. I wanted to get part way up before setting up camp to knock off some of the ascent that day.

I felt this internal struggle. I'm a people-pleaser, and I was worried that if I didn't stay near Paige and Pablo, they'd be disappointed because they seemed so excited. But I had planned to keep hiking and to get more mileage completed. I had to remind myself that I needed to stop pleasing other people. They'd understand that I wanted to get more mileage and wouldn't take it personally. I tried to find Paige and Pablo up on the rocks from where they shouted from to tell them I was going to continue hiking, but couldn't find them. I kept hiking and hoped I'd see them again.

When I came to the end of the meadow, a group of five or so middle-aged men were setting up camp. They were setting up close to the river in a section with lots of tall green grass. I stopped to talk to them about the trail ahead.

As I was standing there talking, lots of tiny bugs were surrounding the grass and flying around. Even though camping on dirt stinks at times, it's better than having bugs all around. I thought to myself, *You're not supposed to set up on vegetation. It's against the rules. You kill those little bugs and their habitat.*

It started to get dusk because we were in the meadow,

and the sun was behind the mountain now. On the map, I saw some campsites near a footbridge, but the terrain was about to start climbing pretty aggressively.

I asked the men how far it was until the footbridge. They said, "About two miles, but it's all uphill. We came down the mountain, and we were flying. It will take you at least two hours to get up there."

I really wanted to cut some mileage and incline off for the next day since Donahue pass is at 11,000 feet, and I was currently at 8,900 feet. I decided if I hurried, I'd make it before it was dark.

The men were not exaggerating. The climb was intense, with lots of rocks and trees and non-stop climbing. I was feeling several blisters on my toes at this point but took some Advil. I was motivated to rise and make it to the footbridge for a few reasons:

1. There was no turning back now because there was nowhere to put a tent.
2. I wanted to cut mileage for Donahue Pass.
3. I didn't like that those men implied I should camp at the bottom near them because it was too steep and too late in the day to attempt the climb. I'm pretty stubborn and was determined to make it before dark.

As I climbed, the trees would occasionally open up and give a beautiful view of the yellow meadow below. It felt good knowing I was down there earlier, but I was making progress.

Just before the footbridge, there were three men and

one woman (in their 50–60's) setting up tents in a relatively large flat area, under trees. I briefly chatted with one of the men from afar, and I asked about the camping situation. He said I was welcome to camp there, but they thought there were more spots ahead. I wanted to see if Tom from Tuolumne Meadows was there, so I kept going. I saw a couple of other tents to the right and left, but it didn't look like Tom's tent. I saw an orange tent like Tom's, but the guy near it didn't look like Tom from afar.

I got to the bridge and crossed it. There was a tent set up just across the bridge with a man and woman. I continued past them to the left on a side trail and found a flat spot where I could set up my tent. It felt secluded enough that trees were blocking my tent a little, and I was not directly off the JMT. But I could still see the tent from the couple nearby.

It was about 6:00 pm, and I started to set up camp. I

went down to the river to get some water to filter. Before I could get down on the rocks to the water, the man I briefly talked to about sites was on the bridge. He looked to be lounging, going for an evening walk. We introduced ourselves, and he said his name was Thomas.

I almost died. I had met a Justin, a Tom, a Justin, and now a Thomas. I don't know why, but things like that make me laugh. Thomas was 66 years old and from Lake Tahoe. The two other guys he was with (Tom and Jerry) were 66 and 69, and the woman he was with (Chresten) was 53. They were hiking the JMT southbound, but started in Tuolumne Meadows. I was impressed that they were embarking on a journey at their age. They were all in good shape and looked like experienced hikers and backpackers.

We chatted for a bit, and then I went down on the rocks to get water. I made dinner, and the couple nearby

were in their tent. I found two trees at my campsite that I could tie my rope around and hang my clothes to finish drying since they hadn't thoroughly dried the day before. I really hoped my socks would dry. I hung up my clothes and cleaned off my Jetboil. I put my bear can about 40 feet away. Being the first night without a bear box, I was very nervous that a bear would smell my food and try to get into it.

I tried to remember everything I read, like not putting the bear can near a cliff or a hill where a bear could roll it away and into a river. I also made sure not to wedge it between rocks or that would give a bear leverage to possibly get it open.

I got in my tent and journaled a bit using the light that I hung from the hook inside my tent. My whole body hurt; my shoulders from the heavy backpack, my back and legs from the climbing, and my feet from the blisters.

As I did each night, I set up my sleeping pad and sleeping bag on one side of my tent and put my shoes, water filter, and backpack on the other side. The tent was very small, but I could sit up in it if I were in the middle. I kept all of my stuff inside my tent because I had read that sometimes chipmunks and squirrels want the water, and they chew through your hydration pack or filter.

I also didn't want bugs inside my shoes. I used my solar charger to charge my iPod shuffle and my watch for the next day, but the watch didn't always charge to a complete 100% and kept dying before I got to my next campsite. It uses a lot of energy, but knowing the mileage and elevation were comforting to me.

- ➤ Camped at 9,600 feet
- ➤ Hiked 11–12 miles

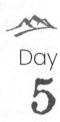

Day

5

Scariest Night of My Life

It was cold the night before, and I didn't want to get out of my sleeping bag. I finally got out at 7:30 am, and the couple near me was already gone. I didn't even hear them pack up.

One thing I noticed each morning on the JMT is that I had to go poop right away when I woke up. It was very consistent, and as days went on, it became more and more urgent. I was thankful that the couple nearby was gone because there weren't many places to go poop where nobody could see me. I wasn't far from the trail, but thankfully everyone was gone, and it was too early for anybody to have climbed that high yet.

For breakfast, I had powdered eggs for the first time. Previously I had dehydrated eggs or oatmeal for breakfast. I had to mix the powder with water and *slowly* bring them to a boil.

Well, a Jetboil does just that; it boils. And it works extremely fast. I ended up burning my eggs but ate them anyway. They were not very tasty. I couldn't clean my

Jetboil very well with just water and my washcloth, but I thought it would do.

I made the mistake of cooking my eggs before my coffee. I boiled water in my semi-clean Jetboil and ended up with burnt egg flakes in my latte. It was better than not having coffee, but that taught me to always boil my water for the coffee before making food in that same pot.

Putting my contacts in that morning was brutal because it was so cold. The trees were blocking the sun again, but my clothes *mostly* dried.

I packed up and set off. Everyone around that area was gone, of course. I wore shorts and a T-shirt because I figured it would warm up again, but it didn't for several hours.

The trail immediately was ascending a mountain. As I climbed, I ran into a woman from Australia, Sharon. She was tall, fit, and in her 30's. She was struggling a bit but seemed okay overall. I would pass her, but when I would stop to take breaks, she would catch up. We did this leapfrogging frequently. I couldn't imagine traveling all the way from Australia to hike the JMT. The jetlag must have been brutal.

I also ran into a woman named Monica. She was an architect from Los Angeles. She seemed to be in her late 20's to early 30's. She was doing a section hike until Red's Meadow, which was at mile 60. I also went back and forth seeing her since we'd pass each other when we stopped to take breaks.

The trail was rocky and, at times, had stairs made from the rocks. Some of the stairs were very large and were challenging to get up and down.

My trekking poles were handy in these moments; they were instant handrails as I slightly jumped down from the larger rocks.

After climbing down some steps, I came across a clear lake with a hint of blue/green. It was beautifully set in a small valley. As with most of the lakes and rivers, there were rocks that I used to cross. Again, the trekking poles made these crossings pretty easy. They ensured that I had balance and didn't slip off the (often) wet rocks.

After crossing, I took my backpack off and got my jacket out. It wasn't warming up much, and there was a lot of wind. My jacket was lightweight, thin, and great for rain and wind. I made a protein shake and drank it by the lake.

Monica and Sharon were traveling alone but were becoming friends. They passed me as I was drinking my shake. I followed behind them shortly after they passed.

The following section was the last bit to the top of Donahue Pass. The trail suddenly turned into large, sharp, steep rocks. The trail disappeared. A few other people were hiking up, and each of us had to keep taking breaks to breathe. I asked one guy, "Where is the trail?"

He said, "I think it's just rock climbing at this point." I kept climbing the rocks and made it to the top, with lots of heavy breathing.

When I got to the top, I saw Thomas and his crew there. He took a picture of me by the sign at the top. I sat on a rock by them and took off my pack. I put my pants on over my shorts because the wind made it very cold. Thomas thought it was funny that I didn't have pants on during the climb because of the cold.

It was gorgeous at the top. I had views in both directions of the mountain range that stretched for eternity. I walked around to take pictures, and a few groups were taking a break at the top too.

A young guy who was going northbound said, "We had to climb, but you guys going south *really* had to climb." I said, "Yes, yes, we did." I felt justified in believing that the climb was not easy.

Monica and Sharon arrived at the peak 20 minutes after I did. Shortly after they arrived, Thomas and his crew packed up to head down. I was also ready to depart. We all headed down, along with Monica and Sharon. I was hiking faster, so I passed them and put on my headphones.

About two miles later, there was a meadow, and it got warmer. My blisters were screaming at me, so I stopped at a creek, got water, ate, and took off my pants and jacket. I bandaged up my blisters because the bandages I put on in the morning were rubbing off. At this point, I had a massive blister on my left big toe and several blisters on the tips of several toes on both feet.

I also reapplied my sunscreen. I hadn't needed bug spray since the second day, but some bees and bugs were flying around when I stopped for water—nothing too extreme, though.

All of this took a while, and I thought, *Nothing is easy in the Sierras. Everything is work.*

Monica, Sharon, and the crew all passed me while I was bandaging my feet. Thomas stopped to talk to me and make sure I was okay. He was a nurse and had some excellent tips for me. I kept debating on popping the large blister but was worried because of the dirt in my shoe. I didn't want it to get infected. Thomas agreed and told me not to pop it. But every single step was painful. I took more Advil, and it helped a little.

I continued and passed Sharon and Monica a few times. At one point, I passed Monica when she was alone, sitting on a log, under a tree canopy. She wasn't doing very well. She admitted she hadn't planned very well, and her toenail was coming off. She was trying to re-bandage it and was debating on tearing off her black toenail.

She showed up a few days before at Tuolumne Meadows and got a walk-up permit. I felt awful for her because her boots looked stiff, and she seemed to be in a lot of pain.

I continued hiking and wanted to make it to Thousand Island Lake because I heard it was beautiful. I got there around 6:00 pm, and it was a vast lake. I saw some people fishing about halfway around the lake. The top of the mountain peaks surrounding us still had snow from last winter in the divots and craters that didn't get much sun.

There was a sign about a rule that you can't camp within 300 feet of the outlet at Thousand Island Lake.

The lake was off to the right side of the trail. I had to climb many rocks and went to the south side of the lake since that would put me closer to the JMT and where I'd have to continue in the morning. I struggled to find a spot where I could set up my tent. There were giant flat rocks, but my tent stakes couldn't go into rock; it needed dirt. I climbed up higher and found a small flat spot on a ledge.

I could occasionally hear a couple and their dog barking above me to the east. I couldn't see the couple or their tent and didn't hear them any longer after a while. I don't know how close the couple was.

I was thankful I had enough water for dinner because it was pretty far down to the lake, and it was getting dark. As I was setting up my tent, a young couple hiked by and were also looking for a spot. They continued down to the large rocks farther away from me and closer to the water.

My campsite had a large rock that I used to cook on

and could lean on. As I cooked and ate dinner, the sun was setting. I put on my coat and pants as it was getting colder.

I was finishing my dinner and watching the stars when I heard that couple by the water cooking in the dusk while talking. Their voices echoed up the mountain, and I don't think they were aware that I could hear them word for word as if they were right by me. It was bizarre because they were far away, and I could barely see them. Here's a bit of their conversation:

Guy: "When did you know you loved me?"

Girl: "I knew you were *different* after one week."

Guy: "Thanks." (sarcastically)

Girl: "No, I mean, I knew my feelings for you were different in a week. Actually, a little less than a week. We had that party, and you came to my room in the morning and stood in the doorway. You had one pant leg rolled up, and you asked if I wanted breakfast. I just knew I really cared about you, and you were different. Then I got scared. *Really* scared. You know, having *those* feelings."

I thought that was a sweet conversation, and it was so true how love works. Sometimes you fall for someone *hard*, and it scares the crap out of you.

I tried to spend some time leaning on the rock, watching the stars, but the cold was setting in, forcing me to jump into my sleeping bag. I put my thermals on and got inside my bag. I couldn't journal because it was too cold. This night became one of the worst nights of my life.

My teeth were chattering nonstop from the cold, and I kept telling myself my thermals would warm me up soon. For 30 minutes, I couldn't stop shivering or shaking, and my sleeping bag was rated for ten degrees. I put my pants and coat on over my thermals and put socks on. I buried my head inside my bag and stuck my mouth out for air from time to time. The air was so cold; it was hard to breathe.

I even had to put my solar charger and watch inside the bag so the watch would charge. I had also read that water filters can freeze, which could ruin them or make filtering impossible, so I put my water filter inside my sleeping bag too.

This cold front appeared rapidly. The wind kicked in, and I could hear it coming through the trees, like an ominous villain coming to get me. Once the wind raced through the trees, it would hit my tent. It shook my tent vigorously on both sides, and it felt like I was going to blow off the ledge.

The wind made its way into my tent under the rain flaps, and I couldn't stop it. My tent was only rated for three seasons. It wasn't designed for winter.

I started to panic because my trekking poles were balanced against the large rock, and I was afraid the wind would blow them off the ledge, but it was too cold to get them. The poles were my most valuable pieces of equipment, and I couldn't imagine making the trail without them.

The wind came barreling through every five minutes from 9:00 pm until midnight. I was frightened and said to myself, *If every night is like this, I won't make it.* The bitter cold was painful, but the wind was just plain terrifying. It felt like a tornado was hitting me over and over again.

The months leading up to the JMT were some of the hardest months of my life, separating from my husband of nine years. I had some very dark times, feeling all alone and worthless. When my husband and I met, he was only 20 years old and was still in school. We worked together at the time, and I was his boss's boss. I had already graduated college (I was five years older than him). After just over a year of dating, he proposed, and we planned our wedding a year later. He was juggling school and work, and he was set to graduate a year after we were married.

After we got married, he moved into my apartment. I never saw him doing homework and would occasionally ask him about it. He said he did his homework when I was at work. We worked at different companies, and he often worked an evening shift and went to school in the morning, while I worked during the day, so I believed him.

I also realized he never talked about classmates, so I'd ask him about it. He'd then tell me about classmates. When I asked what he was learning, he would tell me things he was learning.

I couldn't put my finger on it, but something always felt off. I used to call my husband the "phantom schooler" because I never saw him do homework or heard him talk about school until I asked. But life got busy, and I would carry on. Plus, you're supposed to trust your husband, so I did.

Finally, one day in February, about nine months after we got married, I realized he was supposed to be graduating in a few months and hadn't even talked about graduation. I asked him about it, and he gave me vague answers. I told him, "I want to see your school schedule." He replied, "Right now?"

"Yes," I said sternly.

"I'll have to log on to the website." He walked to the computer in our bedroom. "Oh, I don't have the password. My mom has it because she pays for it."

Noticing something was wrong, I insisted, "Call her for the password."

Nervously, he said, "Now? But it's 10:30 at night."

I saw his hands shaking on the keyboard, and that's when I knew he wasn't in school and had been lying. I responded, "Yes, call her right now for the password."

His voice quivered, "I'm not in school."

I angrily asked, "How long have you not been in school?!"

He responded, "Since we got engaged."

I gasped, "That was two years ago! How could you lie to me? You just made up a fake life. What were you doing when you said you were going to school?"

My husband replied, "Sometimes I'd go to my mom's house. Sometimes I'd stay here if you were at work."

I felt sick to my stomach. "I hate, hate you so much for this. I want nothing to do with you!" I had never said anything like that to him before. I pushed him out of the room and locked the door. I collapsed on the bed and sobbed. I said to myself, *I can't get a divorce. It hasn't even been a year. I can't be one of those people who doesn't even make it a year.*

I felt overwhelmed with betrayal. The person I was supposed to trust with my life, the person whom I committed my life to, was living a lie. I felt tricked into the marriage. I was made to believe he had passions, drive and was going to have a career. Putting up with his terrible work schedule had all been for nothing. I would always be the breadwinner, and I didn't know that going into the marriage.

I felt like a fool for believing him. I felt like an idiot for not seeing it sooner. I figured he must have been laughing at me when I called him the "phantom schooler," all along knowing he was lying to me.

The next day, my husband had flowers delivered to my work and came to see me during my lunch. He said he didn't think I'd be with him if he wasn't in school, so he lied. I asked what he thought he'd do when it was time to graduate. Didn't he think this through? He said, "I didn't think about it. I thought I'd deal with it when the time came."

I tried to forgive him, but we never actually dealt with the issues. His sister told me that he called their mom that night, and they were afraid he was going to hurt himself. I didn't want him to hurt himself, so I tried to forgive him.

For years after that incident, he would attend some classes online and some at a local community college, but he would attend one to two classes and then not go again for one to two years.

My husband knew how sensitive the topic of lying was for me; I had been cheated on in a past relationship. I would occasionally catch him in a lie about something trivial. It would always bother me because I felt if he lied about the small stuff, he would lie about the bigger stuff. I didn't know what I didn't know. Things would be fine for months, even a year. Then something would happen that made me start to question him, and I'd fear that I was being duped again. I felt paranoid.

In October 2015, my husband was promoted after nine years at his job and was sent to Atlanta for corporate training with others across the country. The second night he was there, I realized it was 1:00 am in Atlanta, and I hadn't heard from him. The shuttle would pick him up at 6:00 am, and I didn't want to wake him up if he was sleeping. I used "find my iPhone" to see if he was at the hotel, and it showed he was in a car, leaving the hotel.

He arrived at a bar about two miles from the hotel. I texted him and asked, "Are you still awake?"

He replied, "No, sleeping. So is my roommate."

The fear and panic set in. Why was my husband lying to me? Who was he with? I asked "Why can't you talk?"

About two minutes later, he called me and said, "I stepped into the hallway, so I don't disturb my roommate."

I questioned him, "Really? You're at the hotel?"

He insisted, "Yes, I was sleeping until you texted."

I explained, "Well, I'm going to Facetime you."

I Facetimed my husband, and he declined. He called me, and I asked why he rejected my Facetime call. He said, "I didn't. I don't know what happened."

I sternly said, "I'm going to Facetime you, and you better answer."

He answered and was drunk outside of a bar. My husband started walking back to the hotel. I was yelling at him and asking why he lied. He said he was embarrassed because he was drunk and was walking back to the hotel, by himself, in the cold. I said, "I know you left the bar *because* I called. You weren't walking back to the hotel." He didn't know I used "find my iPhone" so he kept lying, saying he was already walking home when I texted.

I sobbed every night that week, knowing in my heart it was over. I couldn't possibly live with someone that I didn't trust. Someone who had such little respect for me that he was still lying eight years later. But I was terrified to be alone at age 35, and I had never quit anything before.

When my husband returned from Atlanta, I made his mom pick him up after he refused to call her, and he stayed at her house for the night. After one day, I felt guilty because it was his house too. I let him come home, but I was full of resentment. We saw a counselor twice, but she didn't help. My husband started to cancel the sessions because of work and never made an effort.

Now that we were separated, I thought he'd make an effort because he kept saying he didn't want to lose me. But he didn't do anything to stop it. I asked him to get psychological testing to see what was going on, why he lied so much. He kept making excuses as to why he couldn't go.

My husband made me feel unloved, unnoticed, not

cared for or respected, and all alone. There were times after he moved out that I would get very depressed and think, *Maybe I'll end it all at the top of Mount Whitney. That could be poetic. I could use my knife and slit my wrists and just bleed out at the top. All of the pain and sadness I am experiencing will go away. I could just make it all stop right there at the top.*

I'm not proud of the thoughts that would go through my head. But I couldn't talk to anybody about how severe the feelings of sadness and grief were. I knew if I told anybody, they'd commit me. I know this because I watched my brother be institutionalized when he was around 15 years old (I was 12 years old) because he threatened suicide so much. One time, he locked himself in the bathroom with a large butcher knife. I remember being terrified that he would die because we couldn't get the door open.

My brother was hospitalized for ten days, and then he was released because my parents couldn't afford for him to stay any longer. The first time we visited him, the whole family came. He complained about the strict rules and how he had to earn privileges like wearing his hair gel.

The second visit was just my mom and me. We were in a small, dark basement. I watched as my usually tough older brother sobbed in my mom's arms, begging her to let him out, saying the people in there were genuinely crazy and he was only allowed to stay on a tiny circle carpet. He was panicked, saying he'd do anything if she just got him out.

Maybe events during my childhood made me think

about suicide. It seemed to be an option when the pain was too unbearable to handle.

The night at Thousand Island Lake was so terrifying for me, I was afraid I'd die, and now I wanted to live.

I begged God to keep me alive. I prayed for forgiveness. I felt embarrassed and ashamed for even thinking about ending everything at the top of Mount Whitney. I told God that I wouldn't think those things anymore if he would just save my life that night.

I will never forget that night—the bitter cold, the wind, and the feeling that I would die. I begged God to save me and give me peace and comfort—for God to take away my pain and fear.

➤ Camped at 9,847 feet
➤ Hiked 10 miles

Day

6

Fire!

When I woke up in the morning, I realized that I finally fell asleep and was warm. I survived the night.

However, I knew the sun wasn't hitting my campsite, and I didn't want to get out in the cold. At least I wouldn't have to put on clothes because I had my pants and coat on over my thermals. I laid there until around 7:30 am and finally got out of my sleeping bag.

It was freezing outside, literally. There was frost all over my tent, and it made me feel justified in feeling unbearably cold. I went to the bathroom, grabbed my bear can, and came back to my campsite. I put my gloves on and boiled water in hopes it would warm me up. I made my latte and wrapped my hands around the cup to warm them, but it didn't work. It was just too cold. I had to put my contacts in, so I had to take off my gloves and use some Purell. My hands shook, and the cold air gave my hands a piercing pain.

The whole morning was frigid as I tried to eat breakfast and pack up; all I could think was, *I wasn't prepared to hike in the winter. I am getting a room at Red's when I arrive.*

I was trying to wait to pack up my tent until the sun hit it so the frost would melt. I didn't want to pack it up all cold and wet. However, I needed to start hiking to warm up. I packed up and stopped at the lake below my campsite to fill up on water. The sun was finally beginning to reach me, and it felt amazing. The sun's rays felt like a warm blanket.

I hit the trail and continued hiking. I passed several picture-perfect lakes. The colors were a slight blue/green color and completely clear near the banks.

There is rarely a sign on the JMT, so most of the time, I had no idea which lake I was looking at or hiking next to. Occasionally the map would give the name of the lake, and gauging by the size of it and the mileage I completed, I could figure out which lake it was.

The first really large lake I came across after leaving Thousand Island Lake was Garnet Lake. This lake was so beautiful that I wished I had camped there instead of Thousand Island Lake. The trail at times wrapped all around one of the lakes, giving a view of the lake for about three-quarters of a mile.

At Garnet Lake, I saw a couple in their 40's filling up their water. There was a bridge at the end of the lake that helps people cross over a giant rock. It was only about 18″ wide and had a wooden railing on the left side. I crossed the bridge but couldn't see if I was supposed to go to the left or the right because there was no trail, just a large rock. I could make out a trail to the left, so I started following it, but within a few minutes, I realized it was a small trail to get water in the inlet.

I turned back, and when I got back to the bridge, a guy was taking off his pack to get water. We chatted a little about the trail and how it wasn't very clear because it should be to the right based on the map.

The couple I had seen earlier came over and were pretty wild. They were very excitable and couldn't wait to tell us about the Christmas lights they found. They found them on the trail, and each night would put them around their tent or a nearby tree. I guess it had a battery pack. They joked how they'd never bring such an item because of the weight, but they were so thrilled to have these lights. They said if I camped near them, they'd love to have me over, and I should just look for their Christmas lights.

The couple and I continued hiking together for about 15 minutes. I figured I'd follow them for a bit so I could find the trail again. We talked about people we had met on the trail, and they said they had met a woman named Sharon from Australia, but she was having terrible stomach pains and altitude sickness. The last they saw her, she was headed down the mountain. I hadn't seen her that day, and I hoped she was okay. The couple was hiking quickly up the trail, so I fell back and let them go ahead.

The rocks continued on the sides of the mountains. They were huge, jagged, and looked like they had been carved or sculpted. At times, the trail was just jagged rocks, which really hurt my feet. The trail climbed a bit and then down for a descent.

The first few days were mainly all climbing, but now I had to go down too. Up and down, every day. Going down a mountain is not as easy as you'd think. It's very hard on the knees because of gravity. Some of the drops you have to make are pretty significant, almost like jumping off rocks (with a huge, heavy pack on). I used my trekking poles as instant handrails. They helped tremendously to take off the pressure.

Every time I climbed down, I would get disappointed because I had *earned* that elevation. Plus, I knew it would mean even more climbing once I arrived at the bottom.

I came across Shadow Lake, and it was the most beautiful lake I'd seen so far. It was surrounded by mountains and was sort of in a valley. The water was clear near the bank, and there were giant trees that had fallen, just lying in the water, beneath the surface. Surrounding the lake were huge pine trees. I wanted to camp there, but there wasn't any flat surface area to set up my tent. I had dropped to 8,810 feet, and as soon as I passed the lake, it was a climb.

The switchbacks didn't stop, making the climb difficult, physically and mentally. There must have been over 40 switchbacks. It kept teasing me that I was close to the top because I could only see part of the way up.

Two and a half miles and 500 feet later, I arrived at Rosalie Lake. As I approached the lake, I saw a guy setting up his tent about 40 feet below, through the trees. I didn't know if there was additional camping available around the lake, so I thought I'd check out the area where he was.

I had to climb down the hill, and just past his tent was the lake. There were a couple of spots to set up a tent, and as I got closer, I could see it was just him. I got a good vibe from him, so I asked, "Is there room here?"

He said, "Yeah, it's a great spot."

I saw a flat spot about 35 feet from his tent. There was also a fire pit made with rocks, right up against a huge rock. After freezing the night before, I decided this was the spot. I exclaimed, "Oh, a fire pit!"

The guy said, "Yeah, I'm collecting wood to make a fire."

I said, "Well then, it's decided. I'm staying here tonight."

The guy's name was Emmett, and he told me the lake was warm enough to wash up; he had just gone for a swim. It was around 5:30 pm, and I was happy to finally have a little time to wash up. I hadn't washed up since Tuolumne Meadows because of the cold water and my late arrivals to camp. I set up my tent and headed down to the lake to wash up.

I had a small towel made for camping that is super absorbent and dries quickly. There was a fallen tree that was halfway on the beach and halfway in the water. I balanced myself on the log and dipped my towel into the lake, and used it to wash my arms, legs, and face. It felt terrific.

The water was still cold, but it wasn't freezing. Occasionally I could see fish swimming around, so I didn't fully get in the water. Plus, it was too cold for that. I was able to clean off my feet, though, which helped me re-bandage my blisters.

Emmett and I chatted a bit while eating dinner. Then it got dark, and he had gathered enough wood for a pretty decent-sized fire. There was a rock next to the fire pit, so I sat on it. Emmett had a small fold-out chair, which was his luxury item.

Emmett was in his 30's, about 5'9", with short dark hair, almost buzzed. I was finishing up my freeze-dried risotto but was struggling to get it down. I didn't care for the taste and just didn't have an appetite. I didn't want to dump it out nearby and risk having a bear or rodents come to get it.

Emmett suggested that I dump it in the lake. He said the fish would love it and eat it up right away. He also told me that the fish in the lakes up there are imported. I said, "What?! No way!" He said it was too cold for fish to live there all year, but people liked to fish in the summer, so they dumped fish in the water by using planes. There wasn't much food for them to eat at that elevation, so they were hungry. I couldn't believe the fish were imported. I dumped my risotto in the lake just at the bank and five minutes later went to wash off my washcloth. Sure enough, all the risotto was gone entirely.

Emmett was hiking the whole JMT but traveling northbound. He hiked the first ten days with a friend, but his friend couldn't get more time off, so Emmett was hiking the rest solo. Emmett and I sat by the fire talking, and I was so incredibly happy to have a fire. You're not allowed to have fires above 10,000 feet, and with the drought in California, I never wanted to risk it, even when I was allowed.

It turns out Emmett used to work at Target as an Executive Team Leader, a Store Team Leader and then helped Target move into Canada. I worked for Target as an Executive Team Leader for five years, so this felt like such a small world. We talked all about Target, the high-stress lifestyle, crazy work hours, and the disastrous move into Canada, which made them lay off 19,000 people, Emmett included.

Emmett grew up in Canada until he was 16 years old and then moved to the United States. He spent time in San Diego surfing and attending college. Then he moved to Sacramento when Target hired him in 2010. In 2013 or 2014, Target was expanding into Canada and relocated his family (he had a wife and two or three kids) to Montreal. He was in charge of a lot of the hiring.

In January 2015, Target announced they were closing locations in Canada. Emmett moved to Lake Tahoe, California, and was working in the finance industry from home. The small start-up he worked for was based in San Francisco. Emmett said he loved living in Lake Tahoe, and I can understand why. I've been there a couple of times, and it's a stunning piece of California in the mountains.

Talking to Emmett about Target and our shared experiences felt comforting. It was just what I needed, and I felt that God provided the fire and Emmett just when I needed them. It warmed my body and my soul.

➤ Camped at 9,346 feet
➤ Hiked 9 miles

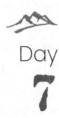

Day

7

Solid Structure

After a warmer night's sleep, I woke around 7:30 am. Emmett said he wasn't an "up and out" guy, and I was happy to see him getting up at the same time as me.

I made some oatmeal and added brown sugar and raisins, while Emmett had some granola with milk. I walked over to his campsite, and we ate breakfast together. I asked how he got the milk, and he told me he brought powdered milk and just added water. He used his little zip-top bag as the bowl. It looked so delicious, and I was bummed that I hadn't thought about powdered milk with granola.

After breakfast, we both started packing up our gear. It made me feel so much better when I realized that Emmett took about the same time as me to pack up—I wasn't so slow after all!

We were ready to head out around the same time but were going in opposite directions. We took a selfie, said our goodbyes, and started hiking.

Shortly after leaving Emmett, I ran into Thomas. I

took his picture in case I didn't see him again. We hiked together for a bit, but then I took off when he sat down on a rock to take a break.

The trail seemed easier now that I had cleaned myself up a bit in the lake, sat by a warm fire, and had some good company. I felt rejuvenated and was hiking fairly quickly. I still desperately wanted a room at Red's Meadow and thought if I got there early enough, I could snag one.

I arrived at Devils Postpile and ran into the other three members of Thomas's crew (Tom, Jerry, and Chresten), so we hiked together for about half a mile. I explained that I was desperate to get a room at Red's that night.

Devils Postpile is a bunch of tall symmetrical rock columns towering 60 feet and is considered a national monument. A few tourists were walking around the area, so I knew I must be close to Red's. I pulled ahead of Thomas's crew, hiking faster to get my name in at Red's.

At 3:15 pm, I arrived at Red's Meadow. There were a couple of old cabins and a couple of old one-story buildings with motel rooms. There was also a backpackers' campground, but you had to walk a little to get to it.

The property included a small restaurant, coin laundry, showers, and a little convenience store. I walked into the store and asked the woman at the counter if there was a room available. She said she had one room left, but she was holding it until 4:00 pm for someone. If the girl didn't show by 4:00 pm, I could have the room. I practically begged her for the room. The woman said that if the girl showed up, I could ask her if she'd be willing to share the room.

Another backpacker heard me saying how cold I was at Thousand Island Lake, and they said they were there that same night and had a thermometer. It got down to 26°F, but with the windchill, it must have been in the teens.

There was a plump leather couch with footrests sitting near the front desk. It looked dusty, so I didn't feel bad sitting there and resting my dusty shoes on the footrest. The woman had given me the resupply bucket that I had shipped there in advance, but I didn't want to go through it yet until I had a place to empty it.

Jerry joined me on the couch, eating an ice cream sandwich he just purchased. It looked so delicious, so I bought one too and rejoined him on the sofa.

He asked, "So, did you get a room?" I told him I was waiting to find out. Chresten, Tom, and Thomas joined us while waiting to get their resupply buckets. Once they got them, the crew headed to take showers and go to the backpackers' campground.

While I waited to see if I could get a room, I started to do some laundry. A man who worked there (he might have been the owner) came to me at 4:30 pm and said the girl they were holding it for didn't show. She stayed in the backpackers' campground the night before, and it was so cold, she wanted to take a rest day there and get a cabin that night. They hadn't seen her around and figured she just headed out and continued to hike.

I was thrilled! The man told me the only room they had available was a cabin that sleeps several people and is usually $220 a night. He said since that's all they had and it was just me, he'd give it to me for the price of their hotel rate: $110. I thought that it was very generous.

I went to grab my load of clean laundry, and the man who gave me the cabin walked over and said he had a couple who asked for a room. He told me I had the option of letting them stay with me, and they would pay half the cost. I hesitated and said I wasn't sure about that.

On the one hand, I was willing to share the cabin with the mystery girl who had the place reserved. On the other hand, I really wanted to warm up, take a shower, go through my resupply, and have some time to write.

I asked the man what I should do, and he said, "You don't know these people. I think you just keep the cabin to yourself." I said, "But I feel bad because if it were reversed, I would be very grateful for someone letting me share their cabin."

The man explained that the couple didn't seem as

desperate for a place, and they were late to the game. He said, "I'm just going to tell them I don't have anything left." I said okay but felt guilty.

The cabin had an A-frame at the front and opened into the combined living and kitchen space. There was a couch, a small kitchen, a hallway leading to the bathroom and bedroom, and a ladder that went up to a loft with two twin beds.

A middle-aged woman was finishing mopping the floor. We chatted outside for a bit while the floor dried. She used to be a guest at Red's Meadow when she hiked the JMT, but she just decided to stay there one day.

I walked into the cabin once the floor was dry. There was a full-size and a twin bed down the hall towards the bedroom. It had a sliding door going to the outside. It was all very outdated furniture with linoleum flooring in the kitchen, but I was grateful for the warmth.

I hopped into the tiny shower and used up the entire little bar of soap they provided. I washed my hair three times because it just didn't feel clean. It had been seven days since I had a shower, and it felt like it. I could not get the dirt to come out from under my fingernails.

I put on my pants and long-sleeve shirt since I had barely worn them, and I needed to finish doing my laundry.

I was able to text my family and let them know I was doing okay. They were grateful to hear from me because they said the Spot device messages weren't always coming through. They hadn't received a notice in days, and when they had received them, it had been spotty. They were happy to hear I was safe.

My family did receive a few messages and location updates. Once I turned on the location feature, it would update my location every ten minutes until I turned it off. Sometimes I turned it on in the afternoon for an hour or two. My dad said, "How come it looks like you're walking in circles?"

I laughed, "Because I was climbing a mountain on hundreds of switchbacks!" The location doesn't clearly show elevation, so it appeared that I was just circling the woods aimlessly.

After sending a few text messages, I headed to the laundry to put my clothes in the dryer. While my clothes dried, I went to the small, rustic restaurant and sat at the counter. The waitress brought me water, and within 30 seconds, I had drunk the entire glass. She said, "Oh, you're one of those," and refilled my glass. I ordered a patty melt with some fruit.

Once my food arrived, I looked around and saw Tom sitting alone at a table behind me. I said, "Oh! I didn't see you there. Can I join you?" He replied, "I had my head down, reading, and didn't see you either. Please join me."

I took my plate of food over to his table, but he was just about finished with his meal. I hadn't talked to Tom very much until this point (it was mostly Thomas). He is from the east side of Washington, the dry side, not the lush green side you think of when you envision Washington state. He went to college at UCLA, and afterward, a lot of his friends moved to Washington, so he joined them. He's lived in various places around the state.

Tom was 66 years old and retired six years prior. He used to be a lawyer, and he worked in workplace injury cases. In 2012, Tom had the idea to hike the JMT after reading a book written by a woman who hiked the JMT and the Appalachian Trail. He brought it up to the guys, but it was forgotten until Thomas brought it up again last year.

Tom told me that he wanted to stay in a cabin, but the others were against the idea, so they stayed in the backpacker's campground. He said, "They think they have to rough it the entire time. I don't get it. That's why they're not here now. They're eating their freeze-dried meals at camp. For me, why wouldn't I enjoy a nice cooked meal at a restaurant if I can?"

I agreed and told him I didn't think we had to "rough it" the entire time. If amenities were on the trail, why not use them? It doesn't take away from the difficulty of the trail and surviving.

The waitress asked me if I wanted dessert and

recommended the root beer float. I told her I was full, but since I hadn't had a dessert in a week, I'd take the root beer float. A woman at a table next to us said, "I admire you. You're full, and you're still getting that."

Tom and I chatted until the place was closing and we were the last people there. He headed back to camp and said he'd meet me for breakfast since the others in his group were going to cook their own. I agreed and headed to get the rest of my laundry.

When I got back to my cabin, I went through my resupply bucket. I sorted what I needed and which items I didn't think I needed. I was grateful that I included another pair of socks since I only started with two pairs.

When I left my house, I had to remove my chocolate bars because I was out of space. I had more chocolate bars in my resupply, so I made sure to add two to my bear canister.

I sent myself a small one-serving bottle of wine that I could enjoy before heading back on the trail. I drank the wine while journaling at the kitchen table.

As I was journaling, a mouse came crawling out from under the cabinets and kept creeping his way towards me. I tried to scare him away, but he wasn't having it. Finally, I got him to scurry away, only for him to continue coming out. I had to put all of my food inside my bear can so he couldn't get it. I thought, *Great, I am finally not in a tent, and I still have to worry about my food. This mouse won't leave me alone.*

I headed to bed but had a hard time sleeping because I kept hearing the mouse's little feet tapping around the linoleum kitchen floor, and I was afraid he'd come for me. At 2:30 am, I woke up sweating. Apparently, my fear of being too cold was a little extreme. I got up and turned down the heat so I could go back to sleep.

➣ Camped at 7,630 feet
➣ Hiked 9.4 miles

Day

8

Sharing Stories

I got dressed and hurried to the small restaurant for breakfast to eat with Tom again. Unfortunately, when I approached the building, I noticed Tom walking away, having just finished his breakfast. I didn't want to bother him, so I stepped inside.

When I saw Tom a day or two later, the first thing he said to me was, "You ditched me for breakfast!" I explained that I was there, but arrived too late.

I sat at the counter and ordered French toast with bacon and scrambled eggs. A young couple in their late 20s sat next to me at the counter, Corey and Brianna. Corey was very tall, around 6'6" with short light brown hair. Brianna was about 5'10" with long, light brown hair. The couple had been dating for eight years.

They were from Grand Rapids, Michigan, and drove Corey's Mustang to California without stopping! They had car troubles on the way, and Corey spent the first day on the trail throwing up. It was much more challenging than they anticipated.

It seemed like the couple had a wild adventure so far! Corey was full of energy and was excited to talk about their experience. Brianna was more reserved and quiet. She hiked in spandex shorts, same as me.

Cory and Brianna were hiking the entire JMT and had started in Yosemite too. They were going south-bound but planned on taking slightly longer than me to finish. They slept at the backpackers' campground the night before.

Corey was a glassblower, and Brianna was a server. It was their first time visiting California.

Once I finished breakfast, I said I needed to pack up and make a phone call. Corey said they'd probably see me out there, so I said, "See you later."

I called Spot to figure out why my family wasn't receiving the notifications that I sent. In the evenings, I had been pressing the button that said, "I'm okay and having a blast!"

The device only allowed for specific functions, like sending those messages, location, or an SOS. One of the two SOS buttons would notify the local search and rescue of my location. They would hike in and help me, so it might take hours or a day to reach me. Another button was harder to access because if I pressed that button, it would send a helicopter.

Unfortunately, the popularity of devices like this meant many inexperienced hikers were pressing that button for things like a sprained ankle or getting lost. This was stressing the local search and rescue, who had to attend to non-emergency calls with emergency services.

The company stressed that the minor SOS button is

for things like a sprained ankle, where you can wait a few hours for help. The button for SOS that was harder to press was for things like being mauled by a bear. If they sent a helicopter for a non-life-threatening emergency, you could be charged $10,000.

I spent 20 minutes on the phone with Spot, and they fixed the issue. My family started receiving the check-in messages again. I was hiking alone, and having that device made me feel much better. It also reassured my family that I was okay.

By the time I packed up and called Spot, it was 11:15 am. I started hiking and wasn't sure where I'd sleep that night. I didn't have a mapped-out itinerary as many people have. Each night, I'd look at my National Geographic John Muir Trail Topographic Map Guide to view what awaited me the next day. I would assess the elevation and mileage, and then I looked for the little tent icon to see where I could camp.

I liked this strategy because it gave me the flexibility of where to stay. Each night, I'd think about how I was feeling, how much mileage I felt I could do, and which mountain passes I had to cross. I knew that I wanted to reach Red's Meadow by day seven, and I had reservations at Muir Trail Ranch on day 12 and day 13. I estimated each day based on making sure I could get there in time for my reservation.

It was a beautiful day with bright blue skies. It was September 7th, and the fall colors were coming out. Grasses and bushes were turning yellow and red. The pine trees were all still green, so I was treated to a beautiful selection of colors.

I crossed over many rivers and streams each day, and this day was no exception. There was always a path of rocks across the water, ensuring my shoes wouldn't get wet. If there weren't rocks, a tree trunk had been placed and smoothed out on top so people could cross on it. I don't have good balance, so I was grateful to have my trekking poles to keep me from falling.

I was also grateful that I didn't have to take off my shoes or worry about raging rivers to cross. People who hike in July have to worry about powerful rivers because of the snowmelt. Each season, people die crossing those rivers and streams because sometimes they can be as high as their chest.

I continued hiking through the mountains and often had incredible views of the mountain range for miles. The trail was drier than I imagined from the books I

read. The dust on the path covered my legs and shoes.

I arrived at a sign for Duck Lake and paused. I wanted to see Duck Lake, but it was off the trail and would require extra hiking and elevation. The Thomas crew said they planned to camp there that night. As I was trying to decide if I wanted to hike down there, Corey and Brianna showed up.

We all decided to hike to Purple Lake, which is directly off the JMT. Brianna looked tired and out of energy. We all hiked together while getting to know each other better. She said the distraction helped her to keep going. That last section was steep and strenuous.

We arrived at Purple Lake at dusk and set our tents up near each other. There were a few logs around that we could sit on while eating.

I walked to the lake to get water, and while it was filtering on a nearby tree, I started setting up my tent.

Corey said, "You have it harder than us. Brianna's going to get our water while I set up the tent. You have to do it all yourself."

I was happy that someone noticed how much work it was! He was right; I had to do it all myself, which is why it always took me a long time. Everything on the JMT is work.

The three of us sat on the logs, eating our dinners in the dark. I told them about my husband, and they were shocked at his lies. They were only a handful of people that I talked to about my husband. It was nice having them there to talk things through.

It was time for bed, so we went inside our tents. It wasn't nearly as cold as it had been, most likely because we were at a lower elevation.

➣ Camped at 10,078 feet
➣ Hiked 14 miles

Day

9

A Life of My Own

I ate my breakfast with Corey and Brianna, packed up, and started hiking with them. The trail was quickly a steep climb. I am slower on the uphill portions, so I told them not to wait for me, and I'd see them later.

Three times I climbed up a peak and back down. The JMT is rarely flat. You're either climbing up or climbing down.

I didn't see anyone for a while, and I thought I had lost all of the people I met. The terrain was rocky, with many mountain peaks looking like sharp arrowheads protruding from the earth.

I didn't see very many animals on the trail. Occasionally, I'd see a deer, but it would run off quickly as I approached. I saw chipmunks and a few squirrels.

If there was water pooled on the trail, there would almost always be 20 bees hovering around it. It always seemed to be in areas where brush made it impossible to go around them. Instead, I just walked through the buzzing. I became so used to the bees; they didn't bother me. They seemed uninterested in me.

I passed several picture-perfect lakes that were deep blue. What made them so spectacular is the mountains that surrounded them.

One time, I was approaching a lake when I saw a man in the distance who was naked and getting dressed. I turned away and talked with someone else on the trail. When I passed the man, I realized it was Thomas! He was too far away to stop and talk, so I kept going.

The next day when I ran into him, he said, "Sorry if I frightened you when I was naked at the lake." I laughed and told him that it was okay.

If I weren't passing a lake, I had views from the mountainsides. The nice thing about hiking the JMT compared to dense forests is that you're treated to views almost nonstop. I was either hiking on the side of a mountain, up a mountain, or on a mountain peak.

I passed rivers and waterfalls. Dave (who took my other permit) told me that after he hiked the JMT a few years earlier, he realized it was probably the most beautiful trail on earth. I had to agree.

Hiking alone for hours a day gives you a lot of time to think. I often reflected on my marriage and our current separation. My husband was included in my group text to my family when I stopped at Red's Meadow. He was supportive and said he was proud of me.

The thing was, I never felt like he saw me. He didn't seem to know me and seemed uninterested in getting to know me. I had been learning and growing over the last ten years, but he stayed the same. My life revolved around him and supporting his dreams.

I never thought of myself as a codependent person. I didn't have a boyfriend until I was 19, and I was always told that I was independent. What I was starting to realize is that my codependency was focused on being a supportive wife. I tried so hard to be a great partner. I wanted to be a good wife, someone who my husband could be proud to be married to. The problem is that I lost myself.

I get joy helping people discover their passions, but it wasn't reciprocated. I've taken the Myers-Briggs personality test, and it says, "Making others' goals come to fruition is often the chiefest concern of Protagonists, and they will spare no effort in helping their partner to live the dream. If they aren't careful, though, Protagonists' quest for their partners' satisfaction can leave them neglecting their own needs, and it's important for them to remember to express those needs on occasion, especially early on."

I was so focused on helping my husband find a career that was good for him, that I often neglected my own dreams and desires.

I also trusted him too easily. I saw red flags during our engagement, like when he lied about what movie he saw at the theater with friends. But it seemed crazy to end an engagement over a film, so I ignored those red flags.

The Myers-Briggs assessment also states, "The interest Protagonists have in others is genuine, almost to a fault—when they believe in someone, they can become too involved in the other person's problems, place too much trust in them."

On the trail, I was finding a life of my own. I was able to meet people as myself, not as a "married couple." I could talk about whatever I wanted. I didn't have to feel obligated to engage my husband in conversation (who was usually quiet in group conversations). People met me and got to know me. I didn't come to them as a couple; I came as me.

I had read about my personality type many times before the trip, so I took the time on the trail to reflect on my actions and things that I could have done differently.

We were separated, and I still needed to decide if I wanted to make the marriage work. I was finding myself thinking less and less about my husband. Sometimes, I had daydreams about a documentary that I wanted to make about the lack of diversity of thought on college campuses. I got excited about the idea that my future wasn't set. I could still decide to change course and follow my passions.

As I hiked through long sections of straight inclines, surrounded by small rocks, my watch died. According to the milage at that time, I should have made it to Silver Lake, where I planned to camp.

I couldn't see a lake or any place to set up a tent, and it was turning to dusk outside. My watch was a very high-quality Suunto with GPS tracking, and it always showed that I hiked more than what the map said. My body also told me that I had hiked more than what the map indicated.

I worried that I passed the lake, lost in thought. I tried to reassure myself that I hadn't passed a lake for some time, and it must be around the corner.

According to the map, Silver Pass Lake was only .6 miles after Silver Pass. I had already climbed up and over the pass, and there was no lake in sight.

Thankfully, after about a mile, I saw the lake at 6:45 pm. It was off the trail and farther down, past some rocks. The campsites were mostly at the end of the lake. Large, smooth, semi-flat rocks surrounded the lake.

I found a spot with a two-foot-high, 20-foot wide rock that would work great for my table to cook on and have somewhere to sit. I started to set up my tent and noticed Paige and Pablo nearby! I thought I had lost everyone, but they pointed across the lake and said Corey and Brianna were over there.

Corey waved and shouted to me, and I waved and

shouted back. It was already late and getting colder, so Paige and Pablo got inside their tent. I walked back to my tent and started cooking dinner.

I hung my small, round light on a tree branch, and it worked well to light up my dining space. It was chilly outside but nothing unbearable.

I couldn't help but notice the bright moon. The full moon would be in eight days, and each night it got more prominent and more radiant. I could see the moon so clearly, and it turned the mountains into a beautiful shadow range. I tried to capture it with my camera, but it didn't show the boldness of the moon.

➣ Camped at 10,386 feet
➣ Hiked 9–10 miles

Day

10

The Possibilities Are Endless

As I cooked my breakfast, ants crawled in a line on my table/seat rock, forcing me off of it. I hadn't seen many insects on the trail so far; maybe it was because of the elevation.

Paige and Pablo were already gone, and Corey and Brianna were across the lake—too far to talk to them. Once I was all packed up, I started hiking.

The view was incredible! The jagged mountains looked like a postcard. It was hard to believe I was standing there. Nobody could see this view unless they hiked in. It was rewarding knowing that you couldn't drive there. You had to hike in.

I was in John Muir Wilderness. I came to a junction with a sign to Vermilion (VVR). I wasn't too familiar with VVR, but I knew it was another resupply option with a campground.

I chose not to send anything there since I picked up a resupply at Red's Meadow. It was a distance off of the JMT, and I hadn't planned to go there. However, I was running ahead of schedule. I didn't need to be at Muir Trail Ranch for a couple more days.

I took my backpack off and got my map out to figure out if I had time to go there. As I was trying to decide, Corey and Brianna appeared. I explained that I was debating on going to VVR but couldn't decide.

Corey pulled out a coin and said we should flip to decide if we should all go there. One side of the coin read, "The possibilities are endless." We said if that side of the coin appeared on top, we'd go to VVR.

Corey flipped the coin, and it landed with that side up! We decided that it was our destiny to go to VVR.

The trail to get to the boat dock said it was just over a mile, but we hiked at least two miles. Corey and Brianna said they noticed that the mileage on the map was never correct, and they didn't have a GPS. I assured them that the maps and signs consistently underestimated the mileage. I researched this later and found out that the difference in the listed mileage is because of the elevation changes. However, officials estimate that the most the trail is off by is 16 miles.

The documentary, *Mile . . . mile and a half*, was named that because they said every time you ask a fellow hiker, "How much farther?" they will answer, "A mile, maybe a mile and a half." It was always more than that, but it mentally helps people think it is just a short distance.

We arrived at the place where we could catch a boat across Lake Thomas Edison, and a few other hikers were waiting too. Two crisscrossed sticks were placed between the rocks, standing up in the air with an orange Home

Depot bucket on top of the sticks. That was the destination for the pickup spot.

The other hikers told us that VVR's regular boat wasn't running because the water was too shallow at their dock and would get stuck in the mud. Instead, they were operating a small tin boat that only held four passengers at a time.

If we hiked to VVR, it would be five miles, so we lounged on the flat rocks, soaking up the sun while waiting for the boat. Because we had arrived after the others, we had to wait two hours before our turn to board.

There was a middle-aged couple and a guy from Steamboat Springs waiting. Sitting near me was Bolivar. He appeared to be 40-years-old, was about 5'7", and had dark hair with specs of gray. I talked with him and found out that he was an architect in San Francisco, California, but grew up in the Los Angeles area. He had a wife and three kids. Bolivar carried a massive camera in a case that he attached to the front of his waist. He said it was his luxury item.

Bolivar was hiking the entire JMT solo and was also going southbound. He told me that he was craving a huge bucket of movie-theater popcorn. He wanted popcorn and a soda while enjoying the air conditioning and a comfortable chair. It was so funny how we each had random things we missed and were craving; things we didn't expect. I enjoyed the sun and conversation, and then it was our turn to board.

The boat took Corey, Brianna, Bolivar, and me while a few other hikers who arrived after us had to

wait. Bolivar sat in the back near the driver while Corey, Brianna, and I sat on the metal seat toward the front.

Our huge backpacks were piled up at the front and tied down. The driver took off fast and water sprayed from the sides and front. I just hoped our packs didn't fly off!

The boat ride was a treat! It was a nice change from hiking, and I felt like I was on an adventure. The lake was vast and untouched.

The boat driver appeared to be in his 50s, was thin, and had a blonde goatee. His name was Jeff, and we tried to talk to him, but it wasn't easy over the sound of the boat. His work history was random, and he moved around a lot, living a nomadic life. We were curious how he ended up driving the boat for the summer and he sort of stumbled on it. Jeff smirked, "When I make plans, God laughs and says 'I have other plans!'"

Jeff was a fun guy, and I like that God has plans for

us that we might not have any idea about. I have felt led by God most of my life, and it's a fantastic feeling when you lean into what God has planned for you—things like hiking the JMT.

When we arrived at VVR, we climbed up a hill from the lake, and there were car campers, a restaurant and a small store in a wooden cabin, a backpackers' campground, showers, and laundry.

I set up a tent in the backpackers' campground near Corey and Brianna. Then I was ecstatic to shower! They charged for showers, and you only got five minutes. I was thrilled to wash my dirty, tangled hair and get the dust off my legs.

I also bought a laundry detergent packet and walked to the laundry room. There were just a couple of washers and dryers, and I worried that I wouldn't be able to get all my clothes washed before they shut them down for the night.

I put on my pants and long sleeve shirt again since I hadn't worn those much and really needed to wash my shorts, T-shirts, socks, and underwear.

A guy who was next to use the washer asked if I wanted to combine our clothes to save time, money, and detergent. I said sure, and we threw our clothes in the machine. I popped my detergent pod in with his, so we had extra cleaning. It felt a little strange putting my underwear in with a stranger's underwear, but at least they were getting clean. Hopefully, he wasn't some underwear fanatic.

I browsed the little shop with Corey and Brianna, and there was a basket of two-pack pop tarts in silver wrapping. The sign said they were mystery pop tarts because we didn't know the flavor. Corey and Brianna bought a few and said they were going to cook their food at their campsite.

There was a restaurant attached to the small shop, and I wanted to eat there. There were only a few tables, and none were open. I saw Bolivar sitting alone at a table, and he said that I could join him.

I ordered a steak salad and couldn't wait to eat fresh lettuce and vegetables.

Bolivar told me about his hiking experience and how he has tried really hard to get his kids involved in camping and to enjoy nature. When his son, who was now 15, was only about four or five years old, Bolivar took him on a backpacking trip in the mountains. There was snow on the ground, and his son ended up being miserable. Bolivar said that it scarred his son with camping, so now he was careful not to push his two younger kids too hard.

I told Bolivar about my experiences camping as a kid and how my dad was never fully prepared with the right equipment. Bolivar was doing a great job of getting his kids outdoors and realizing they have limits and were still young.

Once we finished dinner, Bolivar said he was going to his tent. There was a big communal fire pit with about ten people sitting around it, and I decided to join them. I met a girl from Miami, a girl from Iowa, a guy from Michigan, and a father/son team from Pasadena named Disco and Dave. The guy from Steamboat Springs was also at the fire. It was hard to remember everyone's name, and I found myself doing what they did in the movie, Zombieland—calling people by the city/state they were from.

Some people were hiking northbound and others southbound. The solo people had all found others who they were now traveling with. We talked about the trail, the constant climbing up and down, and the cold.

I had a good time at the fire, but I didn't feel connected to the people there. They weren't very down to earth and seemed fairly self-absorbed.

I went to my tent but had a hard time sleeping. I kept sliding off my sleeping pad, and the lights from the campground kept me awake.

➤ Camped at 7,670 feet
➤ Hiked 8–9 miles

11

Cheese for Pop-Tart

I decided to eat breakfast at the restaurant and joined Bolivar again. We talked about minimalism and "stuff." I had recently been getting into the movement, and it was eye-opening to see how many items I owned. I didn't think so at first because I'm pretty organized. Once I started to examine everything in my house, I was alarmed at what I had accumulated. Many items and clothing still had tags on them.

I made good money at my job, but all of the spending made me captive to the company. At my job, we used to call it the "golden handcuffs" because they had extremely high expectations. We all put up with that and the high stress because of the money. Then we used the money to soothe ourselves by buying things. It was a never-ending cycle.

Bolivar was an architect in San Francisco, and he liked his job, but he also reflected on how much of our lives we spend buying items and working to obtain those items. We were both consciously trying to focus more on experiences rather than objects, which create cherished memories. I enjoyed hearing about Bolivar's insights. We had a deep conversation, which always fulfills me.

After breakfast, I packed up my tent and refilled my water containers. I carried a 70-ounce hydration bladder so I could quickly drink from the straw attached to my backpack. I also had a one-liter bottle that I kept in the side pocket. I usually added an electrolyte stick to that water and drank it when I stopped for lunch or if I ran out of water in my hydration bladder. In addition, I had a small shaker bottle that I'd add about ten ounces of water to. I used that to make protein shakes as a midday snack.

As I was filling up, a man asked me if I was the one who inquired about a ride out of town. I told him that I wasn't, but I saw Corey talking with the man shortly after that. I asked Corey if he was trying to leave, and he sighed.

Corey said that he and Brianna decided that they didn't want to keep hiking the trail because it was exhausting, and he was too tired of staring at his tent night after night. They didn't think they had another 12–14 days in them.

I told Corey that I understood but urged them to keep going because it would get better. Corey explained that after talking with each other that morning, he and Brianna changed their minds. They were going to continue the JMT, and that's why he was talking with the man. He had to tell him that they no longer needed a ride.

I took the boat to the other side of the lake along with Corey and Brianna. We started to hike the two miles back to the JMT when we came across a guy fly-ing down the trail towards us! We stopped and got out of his way, and he stopped to talk with us.

The guy appeared to be in his 30s, but it was hard to guess his age because his skin was so dry and cracked. He was dirty, smelly, and had overgrown facial hair. He was hiking the PCT (Pacific Crest Trail), which is the same trail as the JMT for 150 miles. The guy asked us if there was beer at VVR, and we said he could buy one. Shocked, he said that he heard he would get a free beer on arrival, which is why he was thrilled to get there (and why he was making the side trip).

I hadn't seen too many PCT hikers because it was already September, and they had a short window to cross through the Sierra Mountains before the snow fell. The entire trail is 2,650 miles from Mexico to Canada.

When I did see a PCT hiker, they were always skinny, dirty, speedy, and excitable. I think this guy was the most excited and enthusiastic guy I saw on the trail! He looked like a kid in a candy store. I guess it was because he was so close to a free beer (or so he thought).

The man continued, and Corey and I cracked up at the guy. We realized that hiking for five to six months in rough terrain meant you'd have to be just a little crazy!

We hiked together for two miles, but then Corey and Brianna stopped for water. I always started my day with lots of water because I didn't want to stop midday to get my filter out and wait for the water to get clean. On day three, I had to do that when I was out of water, and it took 45 minutes.

I continued hiking while they stopped. I hiked alone

for two miles and encountered tons of switchbacks. I thought, *My dad must think I'm walking in circles again.*

The trail constantly changed from thick vegetation surrounding the path to dry dirt areas with more spread-out trees.

After hiking for two miles, Corey and Brianna caught up to me and then passed me because I took pauses to catch my breath. My iPod battery died, so I hiked in silence.

I caught up to Corey and Brianna when they stopped for lunch. Brianna was sitting on a log that had fallen by the trail. I sat down with her, and then Corey came running towards us from the trees with toilet paper and a small shovel in his hand. When you're in nature, there's really no hiding when you have to poop.

I pulled out my smoked cheese wheel with a slight flavor (garlic or something). I used my pocketknife to slice into the wheel and ate it with some meat. Corey and Brianna pulled out their mystery pop tart package. They both scoffed in frustration when they discovered it was s'mores flavored.

All three of their packets had been s'mores, and they said it was their least favorite flavor. I told them that it was my favorite flavor, and it looked amazing to me. They offered to swap a pop tart for some cheese, and I was ecstatic! I was so sick of eating cheese and meat or tuna at lunchtime. I didn't care if it was full of gluten.

Brianna had been vegan for the last year, but she said the cheese looked so good, she had to eat it. The look on her face was pure joy, and she said, "This is the best cheese that I've ever eaten!" I told them to eat up because

I was sick of it. I ate the pop tart instead, and it was the best I had ever had.

So much for Brianna's veganism and my gluten-free foods! When you're on the trail, you get sick of the same foods, and the trade was the best thing for us. We sat on that log savoring each other's food.

We hiked together after lunch, and the clouds started to turn dark gray. After climbing for a while, we came to a peak with some of the most incredible views I had seen on the trail.

It was partly because of the dark gray ominous clouds, but we could see across a valley to another ridge of mountains. The trees near us were massive, with branches in beautiful designs.

There was a clearing, and we walked off the trail to the ridge where there were lots of rocks. One of the rocks was in a small cove and was shaped like a couch. I sat on it while Corey took my picture. I called it my rock-couch. There was even a fire pit right in front of the couch!

We all debated about staying the night there but decided we needed to keep going. Before we left the ridge, Corey took my photo with sweeping views. I stood confident and proud. It's my favorite picture from the whole trip.

The storm clouds were in the distance, and we were hiking toward them. Thankfully, we only got a few sprinkles and were then covered by the tree canopy.

When we reached Bear Creek Meadows, we found a camping spot by a river. We set our tents up about 60 feet from each other. The water was frigid, but I was able to wash the dirt off my legs.

We built a fire that night and sat around talking. Corey kept calling one of the lakes Spirit Lake, so we teased him about it. I got to know about their life in Michigan and how Corey was learning more about glassblowing and selling his work independently. Conversations around a campfire were always welcome.

➤ Camped at 8,957 feet
➤ Hiked 12 miles

12

Unpredictable Weather

The urgency to go poop first thing in the morning was getting stronger each day. I don't know if it was because of sleeping on a more rigid surface, but I had to get my sandals on as fast as possible and find a spot for number two before it was too late. The good thing was that once I went poop in the morning, I didn't need to go again for the day.

The sun peaked its way through the trees and hit the side of my tent, creating a beautiful light display and illuminating my tent like it was a special feature.

I made my breakfast and did my usual—get dressed in the outfit that I didn't wear the day before, pull my hair back, put sunscreen on, and then get to work packing everything inside my backpack.

Corey and Brianna left about 20 minutes before me. Once I was ready, I started hiking. It was warm outside, so I hiked in my shorts and a T-shirt like every day. I only used my pants at camp in the evenings and rarely

wore my long sleeve shirt unless I was doing laundry or freezing inside my tent.

It was a beautiful day, and I crossed over rivers, climbed up smooth flat rocks, avoided mule poop, and enjoyed the day. I needed to get to Muir Trail Ranch that day because I had a reservation.

After four miles, I caught up to Corey and Brianna when they were on a break. They ended up quickly passing me again once they were done with their break.

After another mile, I caught up to Thomas. I hadn't seen him in a while, so we hiked together while catching up about our time. His group was ahead of him. Thomas took lots of small breaks when he saw a large rock on the side of the trail—perfect for sitting. I understood it because I took a lot of mini-breaks too. I would often just stand on the trail for one to two minutes to catch my breath.

Thomas and I were halfway up Selden Pass (10,898 feet), and the sky turned white. About ten minutes into hiking with Thomas, hail started to fall! We both stopped and took off our backpacks. I grabbed my pants and put them over my shorts. It was difficult because I had to take off my shoes but tried not to step in the dirt.

I put my puffy blue coat on and hid under a tree with Thomas. We both put rain covers on our backpacks and set them about 15 feet away from us. There weren't many trees tall enough for us to duck under for shelter, and we were on the side of the mountain.

Within minutes of the hail starting, thunder and lightning were all around us. We both realized we were still holding our metal trekking poles. We set them down by our backpacks and got back under the tree.

I watched the dirt trail become white, covered in hail. The thunder was loud, and I prayed we didn't get struck

by lightning. Thomas and I couldn't help but laugh. It had been such a beautiful day, and the hail came out of nowhere!

We huddled close together under the small tree. Thomas looked at the hail covering the ground and said, "It keeps the dust down." That was true. The dust couldn't cover our legs now.

Thomas pulled out a flask with rum inside and offered me some. I happily took a sip. It was the first storm I had encountered on the JMT, and I was happy to have Thomas nearby. The wind was mighty, and it became a white-out. I didn't think my first storm would be hail; I thought it would be rain.

After 15–20 minutes, it stopped hailing. The thunder and lightning were disappearing too, but the white clouds and cold stayed. Thomas said his group was setting up camp just around the corner, only about half a mile from us, and I was welcome to join them. I explained that I needed to get to Muir Trail Ranch.

I put my gloves on and started hiking. When I rounded a corner and a peak, I saw Thomas's group setting up their tents on top of the hail. I waved but told them I had to keep going. The trail flattened out for about a quarter of a mile before the last ascent to Selden Pass. My hands were freezing, and my gloves weren't helping.

When I was at Red's Meadow, I bought two packages of hand warmers. They're the ones that warm up once you expose them to air, and they stay warm for eight hours. I decided to open a package and put a small square warmer in each glove. Within 15 minutes, my hands and fingers were much better.

I noticed Corey and Brianna sitting under a large tree about 60 feet away from the trail. I walked over

to them, and they had their stove out, cooking instant mashed potatoes with olive oil. It looked delicious! I told them I didn't have the patience or willpower to get my stove out and cook for lunch. They usually didn't either, but they needed warm food after the hail storm.

I continued hiking and climbed up Selden Pass after many switchbacks. When I arrived at the top, I looked around, taking pictures. Suddenly, a girl in her late 20s appeared. She was hiking solo and going northbound. She was part of the Ladies of the JMT Facebook group too. We talked briefly, and I warned her about the hail on the trail. Apparently, it hadn't hailed on the other side of the pass that she just climbed up.

I started down the pass and was shocked when the sun slowly started to appear. There wasn't any hail on the trail, and it was slowly getting warmer.

Corey and Brianna caught up to me, and we hiked together. Brianna was feeling tired, and we all wanted

to escape the cold weather. From the top of Selden Pass to Muir Trail Ranch, it was a descent of 2,541 feet and about six miles.

We passed Sallie Keyes Lakes, which were a few lakes close to the trail. Once we passed those, the path became a steep descent. We were on the side of a mountain going down switchbacks and had views of the valley below.

It was stunning. The mountainside had lush green vegetation growing all around, and the sun started to shine on us. It got warmer in the sun as we reached lower elevations.

The beautiful blue-sky clear day reappeared. I had heard that the sierras have their own weather system, and it is correct. The mountains and high elevation create their own patterns and change rapidly. You can't predict what it will be even a few miles down the trail.

The three of us were all exhausted. We had hiked more than ten miles, up and down Selden Pass, and dealt with a hail storm. I told them they didn't need to continue and could set up camp if they wanted, but I needed to continue because Muir Trail Ranch (MTR) only accepted hikers by a specific time.

I went as fast as I could down the mountain and desperately hoped they wouldn't turn me away for being late. At VVR, I told Corey, Brianna, and Bolivar that I asked friends to send me letters to the ranch, and I was really hoping that I'd receive some there!

It was dusk outside, but we made it to the ranch at 6:40 pm. There was a woman outside, and she let us in the gate. She asked if we had reservations, and I explained that I did. She told Corey and Brianna that they'd have to hike another mile to the backpackers' campground and couldn't pick up their resupply until the morning. The woman quickly whisked me off to the dining cabin. Corey and Brianna were gone when I turned around, and I felt awful that they had to walk to the backpackers' campground. We had all just hiked 14 miles and were exhausted.

The woman told me that she usually shows people around and to their cabin first, but dinner was served ten minutes ago, and she didn't want me to miss it. It cost $225 per night, and I had two nights booked. The price included dinner, breakfast, and sandwich items to make for lunch. I also had access to the small outdoor hot spring bathtub. Even the tiny store was reserved for people staying there.

I apologized to the woman for being late and explained that I got stuck in a hail storm. She said they didn't get a drop there. I threw my backpack off and set it on a wooden bench and went inside the cabin.

The dinner was served buffet style, and there were two long picnic tables crammed inside. It was packed, and they added a chair to the end of one of the tables for me. I filled my plate full of the baked chicken and side dishes. I felt like I was the center of attention, being at the head of the table.

Sitting next to me were Disco and Dave. I had briefly met them at the bonfire at VVR. Dave was in his 30s and was self-employed in business consulting in Minneapolis. His dad was a retired family practitioner and lived an hour outside of Minneapolis. They were also hiking the JMT southbound, but I never saw them except at VVR and MTR.

The cabin was cozy and warm. I devoured the food, and it was tastier than I imagined for a backcountry campground.

After dinner, I grabbed my backpack and headlamp, and the woman showed me to my cabin. We walked past the little shop and followed a path towards the woods. My cabin was the first one in that section.

The door was on the backside and under a porch. I opened the glass sliding door, and the cabin was small. There was a full-sized bed, a nightstand, and a twin-sized bed. There was a tiny bathroom with a toilet and sink, but the water was from the creek, so I couldn't drink it.

The wood logs were a classic cabin, so there were small gaps where the air snuck inside. There was just a thin quilt on the bed, so I still had to use my sleeping bag on top to keep warm. The showers were outdoor, and I'd have to find them in the morning.

Once I dropped my stuff off, I walked back to the hot springs near the dining cabin. Two private springs were like small rock pools with hot springs water inside. There was a wooden fence around it, but I was too paranoid that someone could see me inside, so I kept my shorts and bra on.

The lighting was dim inside, creating a romantic setting. I stared up at the moon and stars, feeling incredibly grateful that I was soaking in the warm water. My muscles were feeling much better.

Once I finished with the springs, I walked back to my cabin and got ready for bed. I had a difficult time sleeping because my toe and left knee were killing me. I took some ibuprofen, but they still throbbed. I also couldn't stop worrying about Corey and Brianna. Did they make it to the campground? They would have set up their tent and cooked dinner in the dark.

Meanwhile, I got a delicious dinner, personal hot springs, and a bed with a working toilet inside. I felt so guilty that I didn't offer them to stay in my cabin, but I know the ranch wouldn't have allowed it. They require reservations because they are very remote. There are no roads that will take you to the ranch; you must hike there. The owners use a bumpy service road that only they have access to in order to bring supplies in once a week. It's why the food is included with the room price. They need to know how many people to cook for and ensure they have the right supplies.

I tried my hardest to let it go, but I am a worrywart at times. I kept waking up, worried if they made it, got dinner, and were able to relax. I felt awful that I didn't have the opportunity to explain what was happening. I was whisked away for dinner and then didn't get to talk to them again. I only hoped that I'd see them the next day when they came to pick up their resupply.

➤ Camped at 7,600 feet
➤ Hiked 14 miles

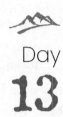

Day

13

Letters of Encouragement

I went to the main cabin for breakfast, and it was buffet-style again. It wasn't as crowded because some people already left.

Now that it was light outside, I could see the property better. I stepped inside the small market, and it was bare bones. You weren't allowed to buy anything unless you were a guest. I asked the guy behind the counter why it was so empty, and he said it was because it was the end of the season. The ranch was going to close up in two or three days.

I saw Bolivar sitting at the computer, checking his email. None of us had cell service, and the last time I had any was at Red's Meadow. I was happy to see Bolivar and to catch up. He picked up his resupply and slept at the backpackers' campground the night before, but stopped by to check his email before heading out. He said, "I saw your name on the list of people who had mail waiting. I'm jealous!"

I was ecstatic! I ran down to the resupply area, and

the guy gave me a stack of envelopes tied together. Bolivar couldn't believe how many letters I received and said it was a good idea to ask for letters. I had posted on Facebook and told some coworkers where to mail a letter, and I couldn't wait to see who sent one and what they wrote.

People asked me what I was going to do with the letters once I read them; surely I wasn't going to carry them back with me? Every ounce counted, especially when you're leaving with a full pack of nine days' worth of food.

I told everyone that I was taking the letters with me! I held the letters tightly to my chest and explained that they were treasures to me, and I couldn't imagine parting with them. I could have taken pictures of them, but I wanted the paper and pen with me forever.

Once Bolivar checked his email, he was ready to head out. I was staying another night at MTR, so we both knew that we likely wouldn't see each other again. We took a picture to remember our time. I was delighted to have met him and wished him well.

I wore my long sleeve shirt (without a bra), jacket, and pants because they were the cleanest clothes I had. I was going to start laundry, but I kept running into people picking up their resupply.

Suddenly, Tom, who I met at Tuolumne Meadows, appeared! I got a big smile on my face and said, "Tom!" He walked over to me, smiling. He said that he remembered how I told him I had two nights reserved to MTR on the 11th and 12th, so he walked over from the back-packers' campground to see if I made it.

I explained that I tried to find him at breakfast at Tuolumne Meadows, but he was gone. Then I always looked for his tent but never saw him. Tom said that he was hiking faster than he anticipated. I got the impression he preferred hiking over spending time alone at camp.

Tom and I caught up with each other about our time spent over the last week and our experiences. He sorted his resupply the day before and only stopped to see if I

was there. He also saw my name on the board for letters and didn't realize letters could be sent.

There was a scale that you could hang your backpack on, and it would tell you the total weight. It's available because people are picking up lots of food and other items. For those of us going south, there wasn't another resupply unless you hiked off the trail. We had to cram all of our food into our bear canisters and ensure we had enough to last 115 miles. Tom weighed his pack, and it was 60 pounds! He sighed and said he wished he didn't weigh it. I decided not to weigh my pack because I didn't want to know how heavy it was. It was a mental distraction.

Tom had to take off, and I knew I likely wouldn't see him again because of my zero-day at MTR. I was able to get a picture of us this time and hugged him goodbye.

I picked up my resupply and started going through a few items on top. A canopy hung over about 30 buckets lined up in a U-shape with supplies other people left behind. You were free to leave items and food there or take what you wanted.

Paige and Pablo showed up for their resupply bucket, and I asked if they saw Corey and Brianna. They confirmed that Corey and Brianna made it to the campground last night. I felt relief that they made it there safely and explained that I couldn't sleep because I felt so bad that I just sort of ran off.

There were hot springs near their campground, but they weren't very nice or roomy. Paige and Pablo had soaked in them the day before.

I continued talking with Paige and Pablo as we all

sorted through the buckets. They were both free-spirits who had positive attitudes and were fun to be around.

When I saw more fancy meats and cheeses in my resupply, I sighed. I told them that I was sick of eating those and didn't want to carry the heavy meat log. Their eyes perked up. They said, "These are the fanciest meats and cheeses we've ever seen on the trail!"

I asked if they wanted some, and they happily took a sausage log and a cheese wheel. I explained that the items were heavy, but they said they would gobble them because they couldn't wait!

It was hilarious because as I browsed the bins, I saw instant mashed potatoes and grabbed a couple. Anything different than what I had sounded good! I rummaged through the buckets, and there was so much stuff. They had everything sorted pretty well, keeping first aid items together, dinners together, breakfast together, etc. I took a few things and figured I'd have to go back to my cabin to empty my bucket and sort it all.

Then, Thomas, Tom, Jerry, and Chresten showed up! They were picking up their resupply buckets and staying at the backpackers' campground that night too. Thomas had freeze-dried his own foods, and his packets took up a lot of space because they were hearty meals.

I asked what it was like the night before because they had camped at Selden Pass in the hail. They said it was cold and not the most pleasant, but they tried to stay inside their tents.

The group had arranged for a mule resupply at Kearsarge Pass. I planned to pick up the pace after MTR because my bear canister could only hold nine days' worth of food, so I knew that I might not see them much after the next day.

We took a picture of the five of us and the picture-taker snapped one right when we were all laughing. Thomas and I were looking at each other mid-laugh when that moment was captured. It perfectly described my time with the group. They always made me laugh and I had a fun time with them.

It felt like a reunion, and my heart was so full. I didn't realize how many people I was meeting on the trail. We were all part of each other's JMT story.

I went into the shop, and it cost $10 for ten minutes of internet time at the only computer there. It was a slow dial-up internet, but I needed to email my friend, Tori, who would meet me on the trail. When I logged on, I saw an email from her saying that the route we planned on her hiking to the JMT, Taboose Pass Trail, was under reconstruction and was closed.

The man at the shop grabbed a colossal map and unfolded it on the center counter to look for alternatives. My friend said that the more she looked into Taboose Pass Trail, the more she realized it was also an incredibly steep, long trail and would be very difficult for her hike up. The map that the man pulled out listed elevation gains, not just miles. I realized that Taboose was not a good option, even if it weren't under construction.

Tori had to hike in on a Saturday, the 17th, after driving to the trailhead on Friday after work. I wouldn't leave MTR until the 13th. The problem is that the JMT becomes more remote with higher passes as you get closer to Mount Whitney. Side trail options are much more limited.

After review, the man and I found Kearsarge Pass. She would have to hike about seven miles, and the elevation gain, while steep, was more manageable. Tori agreed to meet where the JMT and Kearsarge Pass Trail met on the 17th. I explained that I would have to hike 75 miles in five days, with peaks all above 12,000 feet, but I believed that I could do it. I knew I wouldn't have internet again, so I told her to plan on meeting me there. She said she'd bring me some snacks and whiskey.

It was already afternoon, and I still needed to shower and do laundry. I wanted my clothes to dry this time, so I walked to the laundry. It consisted of a wooden platform about a foot off the ground. There were two round, white buckets with a water hose and powdered detergent. I had to put the clothes inside the container, add water and detergent, and then use the crank on the side to spin the container, washing the clothes.

The containers were small, so I had to do two or three loads. Once they were cranked and washed, I had to rinse the clothes. The container had a spout that let water out. I could add water, spin it, and let out the soapy water. This was pretty tiring because it was also low to the ground.

Once the clothes were rinsed, I used the dryer press like what they used a hundred years ago. It worked well at squeezing the water out, so the clothes were now only damp.

Next, I used the clothespins to hang the clothes on the rope stretched across the grass. Thankfully, the sun was out, and it was a small valley, so the sun reached the clothes.

Once I got my clothes drying, I grabbed my shower items. I mailed myself a disposable razor so I could finally shave. The showers were outdoor on a wooden platform. There were four stalls with curtains for privacy. There was a small section before each shower with a bench to put your clothes, but that was also only blocked by a shower curtain.

Thankfully, I was the only person around, and there was hot water. Occasionally, I'd hear people walking by. It was windy, which made me cold, and it would blow my curtains around. I was constantly trying to hold the curtain, so I wasn't exposed. Even with all of that, I was thrilled to get clean and wash my hair. It would be my last shower for nine days.

When I got back to my cabin, a note was on the

mat with a rock holding it down. It was from Corey and Brianna. It read, "Hey! We're sorry we missed you! Pablo said you were looking for us. We feel bad. Hopefully we can see you on the trail. We plan on staying at Evolution Lake on the 14th. Otherwise, hopefully we will see ya before we go! Bri and Corey."

I was happy that they left the note and were okay. They had gone to the resupply section while I was doing laundry and taking a shower. Thankfully, Pablo relayed the message that I was concerned about them!

I used the twin bed to unload my resupply bucket. I sent myself zip-top bags, which helped a lot. I already sorted and repacked the freeze-dried meals before I mailed them, but I needed some bags for trash and the new items I took from the resupply bins. It took me a couple of hours to sort it all and get it to fit inside my bear can. I had to leave several items behind like I did at Red's Meadow. I happily took the extra pair of underwear and socks that I sent.

Then it was time to read my cards and letters. I sat on my bed, slowly reading each one. I cried and was filled with gratitude for the love and support that I received.

Some letters were from coworkers who had become friends and made me laugh. My six-year-old godson sent a picture that he drew of the solar system. One friend sent bandages for blisters.

I was overwhelmed by their thoughtfulness. I cried and laughed and cried again. With their permission, I've included what each person wrote to me. They have good things to say, and I think their words can help anybody who is planning to hike the JMT or has completed it.

Christy,

 Some people only talk about doing something like this. They come up with so many excuses on why they don't have time to prepare; they can't take time off work . . . just so many reasons why they can't do it. I am so amazed that you faced your fears and all the challenges and just did something that you dreamed of doing. You have taken on something that is going to challenge you both mentally and physically. I know that you are going to come out of this an even stronger woman than you were before. I hope that this journey helps you make decisions for your future and really gives you peace and direction.

 I am putting in some quotes here.

  "In every walk with nature one receives far more than one seeks" —John Muir

 I am not only talking about the bug bites, sunburn, and freezing nights here. I am talking about the stars, the silence, the smell of the forest, the beauty of nature, and the peace that you feel.

  "Earth laughs in flowers" —Ralph Waldo Emerson

 I hope that when you feel like crying you could look at the beauty of nature and laugh. It is so amazing!

  "The earth is the Lord's and all it contains, the world, and those that dwell in it."—The Bible, Psalm 24:1

I hope that the Lord has continued to give you strength every day when it has seemed like you are too tired to take another step. I hope this journey has continued to strengthen your relationship with God every single day. I know that you have seen Him in every part of nature that He created.

Lastly, I just want to say again thanks for being such an inspiration to me!!! I am so proud to be able to say that you are my friend. Take care and be safe on the rest of your journey. Please try to enjoy every minute of it. When you come back I would be honored to throw a party for you so that we can all hear about your journey!

Your Friend, Karyn

Dear Brave Christy,

I sure hope this card finds you happy and fulfilled! :) I can't wait to hear all about this adventure—what you saw, what you experienced, who you met, etc. Can't wait to see pics of your journey. Stay safe and fill that journal with all your thoughts so you don't forget them! Proud of you and envy your fearless attitude and brave soul.

Talk soon! Jenny

Christy,

You are halfway through your trip! I can only imagine how difficult this trail has been. I'm sure this rest stop is exactly what you needed. I hope you are enjoying your snacks and enjoying the bed you get to sleep in. Ronda has been checking the weather every day and letting us know your weather conditions, lol (I don't know if she really knows your location, though). Based on what she sees, she says you have had sunny days, so I sure hope that's the case.

We have all been thinking/praying for you. I hope the trail has been treating you well. Two weeks in, and I hope you are getting used to the big heavy backpack, the same food, and getting comfortable in your tent. I seriously don't know how you are doing it. You are definitely a beast! :)

I hope you have found clarity on this trail and pray that God answers your prayers. You are so strong, and I know that you will be okay. God will direct your path and help you get through this tough time. My favorite verse during any of my hikes has always been, "I can do all things through Christ who strengthens me." I hope this helps you as much as it did for me.

Obed's birthday celebration was a hit. Barry Bear actually came through with the Portos delivery. You can only imagine how happy Obed was that day, lol. (Barry even came in early).

Don't worry, Obed and I are getting along, lol. Everything here is going smoothly. Can't wait to hear all about your trip. Take care and see you soon! :)

Valerie

Christy!

I hope this letter finds you well. By now, you've probably seen tons of amazing vistas, and I'm sure you have so much more awesomeness to see! I hope you took hundreds of pictures to share with us. :) I'll keep the work details short—the guide is coming along. I'm almost done with the script. It's been super quiet without you here! I don't like it! I joke with everyone that I could die, and maybe Valerie would find me hours later (which is probably pretty accurate). Barry did an excellent job decorating my desk for my birthday. I felt very special but wish you were here to see and partake.

Everything else is going well. I'm looking forward to brunch on Sunday. I have a ton of questions for you about the hike, but I will wait until you get back. Expect to get bombarded! LOL

We are all so proud of you and know that you will rock the rest of the hike. Your team is rooting for you!! We miss you tons!

Obed

Christy,

God was so good to direct me to your perfect card with a tent, hiking boots, and beautiful landscape just like I imagine you now! Let me say that I am in total awe and admiration of your determination and diligence to achieve this major milestone in your life— not many can say that they conquered the JMT. You will never forget this and will have great stories to inspire your grandchildren one day. Savor every second of this once in a lifetime opportunity.

You are halfway there girlfriend—"You can do ALL things through Christ who will give you strength."

Thinking of you today and the entire duration of your JMT adventure. What an achievement!! What an amazing person you are!! So proud to call you a dear friend. :)

Love and God's blessings, Ronda

Christy,

I'm praying all is going very well! You have probably seen some amazing sights. Can't wait to see the pictures. Have you met many people so far on the trail? Hope you are sleeping well and relaxing when you are able.

If I were younger and in better shape, it would have been an amazing adventure to take with you! Nothing new going on here, but it is Missouri in the summer . . . you know how that is, lol. Enjoy the rest of your trip and can't wait to hear all about it!

Love, Mom

Hey Christy,

So proud of you for what you are doing. What a fantastic accomplishment. I sure hope your hiking boots are comfortable and not like Cheryl's in Wild!

I can't wait to hear your account of this adventure. I'm wondering if you are meeting people along the way. How is your food tasting? I suppose you can have non-camping food now that you are at a rest spot. I'm hoping that this is a really great process for you in so many ways—you have been going through so much physically as well as emotionally. I'm so proud of you for taking this time for yourself.

I can't imagine how beautiful the trail must be—peaceful as well, I hope. Rich and I are going to Bishop fishing next month, but we are staying in a little cabin—I'm not sure I'm as brave as you are!

I just wanted you to know I've been thinking of you, and I'm rooting for you on this journey!

Sending you hope for NO BLISTERS, perfect weather, plenty of food, and finding everything you need along your way. I'm really proud and excited for you. Enjoy!

Sharon

On an Alaska postcard:

Hi Christy,

From our trip to yours! Hope you are having the experience of a lifetime. You are taking getting back to nature, unplugging, de-stressing, and everything else they say to the next level. I look forward to hearing all about the trip.

Julie

Dear Christy,

Hope you're enjoying all the beautiful sites that God has created while you're on your adventure. It's absolutely amazing what you're doing. God bless you and praying for your safe return home.

Mary

Christy,

Congratulations on how far you've come! I'm sure there have been some bumps in the road/trail that you have to overcome—but here you are! I hope you are finding yourself out there and feeling your value and worth in the world.

Stay away from bees and come back with great stories! Onward, my friend!

Trisha

Embrace the suck!

If you are reading this that means you made it to your resupply spot. So halfway-ish. So CONGRATS! You have made it this far and have probably already 'embraced the suck.' Hopefully, your adventure has been filled with more good times than hard times. I hope your feet are in good condition with minimal blisters. I have included a second skin pad. Just put on the site of your blister and cover it with moleskin or a Band-Aid. It's then like you don't even have blisters!! :)

How are you enjoying your time? Are you finding your time peaceful and filled with God's presence? Have you made some friends along the way? Did you meet any bears? If so, I hope it was from afar but yet close enough to capture a bear's stunning beauty in the wild.

I challenge you to spend at least one night under the stars without your tent. You can still set up your tent, but pick a spot that's not on an anthill and where the weather will be decent and try it! Sleeping under the stars is one of my favorite things. You can just fall asleep as you stargaze.

Here are some bible verses that I like to chant when I try to embrace the suck on my trips.

Philippians 4:13
I can do all this through Him who gives me strength.

Psalm 46:1
God is our refuge and strength, an ever-present help in trouble.

Isaiah 33:2
Lord, be gracious to us, we long for you. Be our strength every morning, our salvation in time of distress.

And a favorite because being in the wilderness reminds me of God's creativity in creations.

Genesis 1:1
In the beginning, God created the heavens and the Earth.

I cannot wait to hear of your adventure when you return and see your amazing photos. I will be praying for you while you are on this trip. Here is a prayer also:

Dear Father, we thank you for giving Christy the opportunity to go on a three-week trip. Thank you for providing the monetary resources and the time off work. We pray for continued safety from people and animals, and the elements. We pray that Christy would feel your presence during this adventure and that she would end up feeling closer to you than when she started. We pray that Christy would feel your love, peace, and joy. We pray that you would give Christy clear communication and wisdom on how to handle her marriage. We pray that you would heal Christy's hurts both physically and emotionally. We pray these things in your precious name, Jesus Christ, Amen." :)

Cannot wait to see pictures when you get back!
Debbie

Dear Christy,

We've written, emailed, and texted so much over the years that writing this letter should be easy, but right now I'm at a loss for words. I'm trying to imagine your experience thus far on your hike and I think the enormity of what you're doing has finally hit me.

How are you doing? I hope your pack was a manageable weight and I hope you're not hungry. I hope you've met some amazing people and have had some life-changing experiences. By this point, I bet you've surprised yourself with your resourcefulness and resiliency.

Anyway—favorite moment so far? Biggest challenge? What do you miss about home, besides regular access to showers?

Over the years, you've inspired me many times, and I have always looked up to you (literally and figuratively), but you taking this risk and just going after life—and yourself, in a sense, is just so impressive. You rock! If only I could be out there with you . . .

Anyway, life here is a lot of the usual. My mom is staying with us and looking at properties at Hilton Head—making dreams a reality. It's making me realize that I need some new dreams. For so long, my dreams revolved around having a child, getting my masters, leaving PA, seeing the 50 states. I'm glad I've done these things, but now what? In a lot of ways—and I've told you this before—I feel like I found myself again after visiting you this summer. It's like I'm more confident in myself and care less about what others think. I'm trying to deliberately choose the people with whom I surround myself—and while not always possible, I just want to be around people who make me feel good about myself— and I want to do the same for them of course. But dreams—those used to come naturally but right now I'm stuck. Maybe I'm just living the dream—ahahahahaha.

Anyway, I could bore you with some mundane details about job searching, Miles' school, needed house projects, and so on—but I won't. You're escaping all of that right now, which must be amazing.

Be safe—have fun—and we will need to plan either Vegas or us coming to see you when you return, because I know we have so much catching up to do.

Enjoy every moment! So proud of you!
Love, Misty

Each letter was just what I needed to hear. Their words and thoughtfulness reminded me how blessed I am to have such spectacular, insightful friends. I clung to their words.

Friends knew that I was separated from my husband, and they hoped that hiking the JMT would give me time to think and reflect. They were right—I had a lot of time to think.

I couldn't help but notice the absence of a letter from my husband. When I sent a quick email to my family earlier saying I was at MTR, my husband replied asking if I received his letter, but there wasn't a letter. It made me sad and disappointed and confirmed what I knew deep down—he didn't care about me. He was always the focus of our marriage. I was insignificant.

I didn't want him to take away the joy I felt from my friends who took the time to write a letter and mail it in time for me to receive it. I focused on their words of encouragement and soaked up every bit of advice.

It was time for dinner, so I walked back to the cabin for steak. I sat near a man from San Diego. He appeared to be in his 40s. The man constantly bragged about his accomplishments and how he was an excellent hiker. He seemed like one of those men on Wall Street who thought too highly of themselves. He was a jerk, and I didn't care to talk to him.

After dinner, I grabbed my clothes from the clothes-line and went back to my cabin to repack. I hung a few items up in my place just to make sure they were dry.

I spent some time sitting on my bed and journaling so I wouldn't forget things about the trip. It was challenging to write in my tent each night because I had to sit up, and it was cold. I was able to write at Red's Meadow and MTR, but it was short notes and pictures to help me remember things after that.

There was a giant bug flying around my light, and I kept knocking it away. The couple in the cabin next to me talked about the weather and how cold it was. It was colder that night than the night before. I slept a lot better, though. I was excited to start the second half of the trail.

➤ Camped at 7,600 feet
➤ Zero-day—no miles hiked

Day

14

Purple Hands

I ate breakfast in the main cabin with a couple from Atlanta who appeared to be in their late 30s. They were hiking northbound and said there wasn't much hiking available in Atlanta, so training for the amount of climbing on the JMT was challenging for them.

The woman told me that she started her period at 2:00 am on Mount Whitney, which made her sluggish and was difficult to manage. I received an envelope of pads that I mailed to myself at MTR and expected to start my period sometime during the second half.

The couple tended to hike early in the morning to get over the passes by early afternoon. The mountains that I was about to encounter steadily got higher and higher. The woman said, "You can't hike passes late in the day unless you're a machine." I smiled inside because I was usually on passes in the evening. Maybe I was a machine?

It was time to finish packing up and continue hiking. Before leaving the ranch, I asked an employee if there was any mail that was delivered and didn't make it to my stack. He said there wasn't, but I could leave my forwarding address in case anything showed up after I left. They would only be there another few days before leaving for the season. I said, "I'd appreciate forwarding any letters. I was expecting one that wasn't in the bunch."

The man took my forwarding address, and I headed out. As I was leaving, a male hiker in his 30s was leaving too. We started hiking together, and he explained that he was hiking the whole JMT southbound but had met up with a couple and another guy early on, and they were hiking as a group. He was behind that day because he stopped for some items at MTR, but he planned on catching up with them.

Trevor was from Vancouver, Canada, and worked in construction. I asked what it was like there, and he said Vancouver housing had become so expensive due to Chinese investors buying up properties downtown that locals were forced to the suburbs. Most of the homes he helped build were in the suburbs because of this.

Trevor was married and had a couple of kids. His wife was a kinesiologist and a medium. He said that his wife was very sensitive to energy. One day, they were walking into a hardware store when his wife stopped and said someone was having heart problems. She was concerned, but they walked inside. Shortly after, an ambulance was called because a guy was having a heart attack!

I told Trevor that my sister was a chiropractor, and she does energy work and acupuncture. I know it sounds crazy, but we are made up of energy, so it makes sense that we can sometimes feel the energy.

Trevor and I hiked together for four hours. It was a beautiful day, and we passed waterfalls and walked over a bridge. We even saw a few deer grazing just off the trail. Parts of the trail were steep and full of tree roots, so I had to be careful with my footing. I told Trevor that every time I looked up to see the view, I'd trip on some rock that was hidden under the dirt. He agreed and said we had to pause to really take in the scenery.

I enjoyed talking with Trevor and it helped pass the time. Trevor stopped to filter water, and I kept going. After a little while, I ran into the group of four—Tom, Thomas, Jerry, and Chresten. There was a sloped river on wide rocks creating small waterfalls. I took pictures of it, and then Jerry offered to take a picture of me with the water. I was wearing shorts like always, and Jerry said, "You'll have to put some clothes on those strong legs at some point." They mostly hiked in pants, but pants made

me feel too restricted. I had my jacket on because it was chilly but I didn't want to deal with taking my shoes off to get my pants on. I thought to myself, *My legs are getting strong.*

I continued and then came to a wide, shallow river in a meadow. I wasn't sure if it was the trail, and thankfully, the group appeared. They confirmed it was the path, and we'd have to take our shoes off to cross the 30-foot wide stretch. It was the first (and only) time that I needed to remove my shoes for a water crossing.

I put my sandals on to protect my feet from the rocks, and the water was cold! I crossed the river and the cold felt good on my feet. I was so happy that the crew was there with me. I chatted with Chresten while we took our shoes off and back on. She was a pilot, flying mostly international routes. The amount of downhill climbs were really bothering her knees.

Once I crossed, I sat on a rock to put my socks and shoes back on. The group would stop to camp soon, but I needed to cover more mileage if I were to make it to Kearsarge Pass by the 17th, so I kept hiking. I said my goodbyes because they planned to take two weeks to finish, and I knew I likely wouldn't see them again.

I had already hiked eight miles with a full pack of food and water for nine days, but I wanted to make it to Evolution Lake, another eight miles away and up 2,400 feet.

The trail became steep with never-ending switchbacks. I was getting higher and higher up the mountain range as the sun lowered and lit up the east side of the mountains and created a shadow on the west side.

The sunset was a beautiful sight across the skyline of mountains and trees. However, I was starting to get nervous. I didn't see a lake anywhere and was climbing a mountain. Where was the lake? Did I pass it? Was a lake really this high up a mountain pass?

I kept climbing and started feeling desperate. I was exhausted. The sun was behind the mountain range, and it was now dusk. It got colder with each step of elevation gain, and the lack of sun didn't help. I looked around the area to see if I could just set up somewhere there, but there weren't any flat spots for a tent. It was steep and rocky.

I thought I had reached the top, and it started to level out a bit, but there was no lake. I was still only wearing my shorts and a wind jacket, and my hands were freezing. I didn't want to take the time to take my pack off and dig for my gloves and pants. But then I noticed my hands were turning purple.

I took my backpack off and grabbed my gloves because I kept them in the outside pouch. The pants would have to wait. I needed to get to a campsite before it was completely dark.

Finally, I rounded a corner and saw Evolution Lake to the left! I couldn't believe a huge lake was at the top of the mountain! I started walking quickly to the area where tents could be set up.

I saw a group of four older people standing in a circle talking. They were all completely bundled for winter, wearing coats, pants, gloves, and hats.

I must have looked so wiped out because one of the men walked over to me and said he'd help me set up my tent while I "put some clothes on." I found a spot near a tree and a rock. I was shivering. While the man spread out my tent, I put my pants over my shorts and put on my heavy coat. The man sounded like he was from Germany and said his group was doing a four-day loop, but it was colder than they expected.

Once the man helped me set up my tent, he walked back to his group. I turned on my headlamp and made a freeze-dried dinner. I didn't want to walk to the lake in the dark, and thankfully, I had enough water.

The stars were incredible, and the moon shined so bright that it helped to light up the area. That night, I changed into my wool thermals, put my pants and coat over them, and put wool socks on. I even slept with my gloves on. After the freezing night at Thousand Island Lake, I knew just to wear everything from the start. It worked and kept me warm.

> Camped at 10,875 feet
> Hiked 16 miles

Day
15
Period

I woke up chilly, but the sun was shining on my tent. When I climbed out of my tent, I noticed there was frost on the outside. Another frosty night, and I definitely felt it.

I walked to the lake and got water for breakfast and for the day. I enjoyed my oatmeal with raisins and brown sugar. Surprisingly, I never got sick of that. I think it's because the raisins and brown sugar were treats.

As I packed up my stuff, I saw Trevor walk by, near the lake. I had gotten the impression that he thought he was a better hiker than me. I couldn't really blame him—I breathe heavily when going uphill because of cardio-induced asthma and a deviated septum. I have a very slow heartbeat, and when I start climbing up a mountain, it beats fast, making it hard for me to breathe. I've seen a cardiologist a few times, and there isn't anything they can do.

Trevor had hiked and backpacked more than I had. He worked his way up to completing the JMT, and this was my first backpacking trip ever. I'm sure I appeared out of my element. I was a little overweight and almost always got to camp late. But my tardiness wasn't a reflection of slow hiking.

Once I start hiking, I don't stop much, other than my micro-breaks, where I just stood there for a minute to catch my breath. I usually only stopped for lunch for 20–30 minutes to go to the bathroom and eat. I would find a rock or tree off the trail and sit on that for lunch. Many people that I met started earlier but spent more time during lunch.

They got to camp earlier because of their earlier start. I rarely had time to wash up in the lake because it was dusk, and the water was way too cold. I had read about people swimming in the lakes, and I don't know how they did that. Maybe they hiked in July–August, swam in a lake at lower elevations, and didn't mind the cold. I only saw people in a lake a handful of times during the entire three weeks.

I caught up to Trevor, and we leapfrogged each other several times because we were on different break schedules.

The trail was beautiful, with bright blue skies above and blue lakes. One lake had a rock path with about 30 rocks in a perfect line to use to cross.

The trail was often only a few feet from the side of the lake, so I walked along admiring the water with the mountain as a backdrop.

As I got closer to Muir Hut, the path and terrain were only rocks—a sea of rocks as I climbed to the top. It looked like another planet with no life.

I felt tired and weak the whole day, and the climb to the hut really hit me. I didn't know why I was lacking energy and felt lethargic, but I needed a break. I sat on a

rock and ate my waffle cookie, which I usually saved for later in the day.

Two guys passed me, and then Trevor passed as well. I continued climbing, and then I realized what happened—I had just started my period. There were no trees in sight or large-enough rocks to hide behind. People climbed up and down, so there was no way that I could get privacy.

I arrived at Muir Pass, where the Muir Hut sits at 11,975 feet. I was wearing my wind jacket and shorts. The blue sky was deceiving because it was actually chilly outside.

Muir Hut is a round hut made from rectangular stones. There were a few people inside and outside taking breaks and eating. I thought about hiding behind the hut to put a pad on, but it still wouldn't provide enough privacy.

I went inside the hut, and there was a fireplace that had been filled in with stones. There was a ledge circling the inside of the building. I sat down to enjoy the warmth and to be able to rest my feet. I started eating a

snack while a few other people came inside to take pictures and look around the small hut.

Suddenly, I realized nobody was in the hut except me. I looked through the window and saw a couple of hikers coming up, but they wouldn't arrive for at least a few minutes. I couldn't guarantee that nobody who was wandering around at the top would pop in, but I decided to take my chances.

I quickly pulled my shorts and underwear down and placed a pad before pulling them back up. Thankfully, nobody saw me—not that I'm aware of anyway. If I didn't do it then, the downhill would be the same problem, no privacy. These are the things that women have to worry about while long-distance hiking.

I continued hiking, and the landscape was completely gray. Gray rocks on the ground and jagged gray mountains all around. Occasionally, there were small lakes in the shallow areas. I was definitely above tree-line.

As I descended, more greenery appeared. Raging waterfalls provided signs of life, and I saw three deer in the meadow. Gnats swarmed me in the meadow, which was annoying.

I stopped at Le Conte at 6:40 pm and found a spot for my tent. I saw a couple of other tents nearby but they were through the trees. It was lower elevation than the night before, so it wasn't nearly as cold.

I used the river to get water and to wash my legs and arms off. I hated putting my thermals on when my legs were dusty. Getting the dust off made a huge difference.

I made my dinner and cleaned up. There was a fire pit

at my site, but I couldn't get it lit with my small lighter. I saw a fire going with people around it, so I walked over to ask if I could warm up at their fire for a little bit. They told me to sit down and join them.

It was a group of three men who appeared to be in their late 30s to early 40s, named Jim, Dave, and Chad. They were from Toronto, Canada, and were all police officers. The men planned to hike a five-day loop, but one of the men sprained his ankle on the first day. They set up camp and waited for a mule train to pick him up and take him back to civilization. It took a couple of days, so the other two guys did day hikes while the injured guy rested at camp. I heard that most injuries on the trail are sprained ankles. I understood why—the path was always full of rocks.

There was also a girl with short dark hair, 30 years old, named Sam. She had been a teacher in Connecticut and was moving west. She wanted a life change and was hiking the entire JMT solo, but she had met up with Trevor and the other couple that he was hiking with. They were camping farther ahead and she fell behind. She was short—around 5′1″, but she was spunky and moved those legs very quickly.

We talked about trail friends and what it was like for the officers in Canada. They told stories about how they wanted to help people, and sometimes it was dangerous. They couldn't believe that their trip ended up the way it did after months of planning.

It was two months before the U.S. election between Hilary Clinton and Donald Trump. We briefly talked about politics, but everyone avoided saying who they supported. One great thing about the JMT was that nobody talked about politics. We talked about life, our thoughts, nature, the trail, and adventure. Politics were divisive, and the trail brought people together. We weren't defined by who we voted for; we were defined by who *we* were—our actions and words.

The trail was about our shared interest in the outdoors. It was about all of us surviving in the wilderness. As humans, we instinctively helped each other because the priority was staying alive. Politics were useless out there in our new world.

I enjoyed sitting by the fire and getting to know other people. I slept in peace and quiet by myself but had people close enough that I wasn't scared of being out there alone.

➤ Camped at 8,737 feet
➤ Hiked 14 miles

Day
16

Golden Staircase

I ate my usual oatmeal with brown sugar and raisins for breakfast. Then I got to work filtering water, cleaning my dishes, stuffing my sleeping bag inside the stuff sack, and somehow managing to get it all inside my backpack. Then it was off to the trail.

I climbed up rock steps and then was treated to beautiful views of green pine trees and tall mountains

all around. Each day, the bushes and plants turned more yellow, and some turned red. The fall colors provided a great variety in the landscape.

I hiked alone but leapfrogged Trevor and the couple from D.C. that he often hiked and camped with. I came across Sam, and it was time for lunch, so I joined her on a rock and ate my tuna, cheese, and peanut butter.

Sam had large, round, blue eyes that gave an inno-cence about her. She was smart and curious. Sam had hiked some of the Appalachian Trail before. She decided she wanted a life change and drove from the east coast, stopping in the southwest to hike before starting the JMT. She was using the time to reflect and figure out what she wanted to do in life. Nature is a great place to pause because there aren't constant distractions.

After we ate, we hiked together until we got to the

Golden Staircase, a set of switchbacks that don't seem to end. You can see many switchbacks at a time because there aren't trees, just short bushes. It's a steep climb to the top, and you can almost feel dizziness from the number of switchbacks. It's called the Golden Staircase because the golden hour before sunset can give it a yellow glow from the reflection off of Palisade Creek.

I had to take several breather-breaks to catch my breath before continuing. Trevor, Sam, the married couple from D.C., and an older guy were all climbing but at different paces and different break schedules. At one point, we all ended up close to the top, taking a seat on some rocks for a break and snack while enjoying the view.

The Washington D.C. couple appeared to be in their 30s, and were avid, experienced hikers. The man's name was Mike, and the woman's name was Grove. They had

completed 500 miles of the Appalachian Trail (AT). I felt like a newbie next to them—like I didn't belong on this challenging trail.

I asked how the AT compared to the JMT, and they said the AT is mostly through a forest, so you don't get the constant views that you get on the JMT (like the one we were admiring). With the JMT, we were always on a mountain with views for miles. The AT has ascension, but not to the degree as the JMT, and definitely not the same elevation. The JMT was drier and dustier, which I could agree with.

The older guy appeared to be in his 50s and had hiked the JMT before. He was doing most of the trail again, but not the entire thing. He was also a very experienced hiker. When we reached the top of the Golden Staircase, he congratulated us, saying it was one of the hardest parts of the trail. We climbed about 1,400 feet in two miles.

We arrived at Palisade Lake at 4:45 pm, which was pretty early for me to camp, but everyone decided to set up camp there. There were also two brothers at the lake. I decided that it would be nice to have an earlier evening and not be eating in the dark. Plus, I had company to camp next to.

Sam and I found a spot in the brush that would allow for two tents, so we put our tents side-by-side. Once I set up my tent, I actually had time to use my washcloth at the lake and wipe off the dust again. The water was cold, but at least it got me somewhat clean.

There were massive, flat rocks scattered in the area, and I ate my dinner on the rocks with Sam and the two brothers. When I picked up my resupply at MTR, I included a nice chocolate bar divided into smaller squares. I allowed myself two squares each night so it would last me a few days. It was the one food item that I wish I brought more of. After a long day of hiking, the chocolate tasted like heaven.

We enjoyed the views, relaxing and talking about the trail until it got too cold and windy.

I laid down, and my body hurt everywhere. Perhaps it was the Golden Staircase, but my body ached worse than it had before. My backpack made my shoulders and chest sore, and the hip belt made my hips hurt. My legs were worn out. My knees and feet were throbbing. I took some ibuprofen to help with the pain and inflammation. I made sure to take my calcium and magnesium each night because the removal of two of my four parathyroid glands six months earlier, meant that I needed to ensure my body got plenty of calcium.

My body needed to rest, but I still had two very long days ahead of me if I was going to make it to Kearsarge Pass in two days.

➤ Camped at 10,646 feet
➤ Hiked 10.5 miles

Day

17

Underestimated

I knew it would be a long and demanding day, but I still made my breakfast and latte. While I cooked, Trevor, Mike, Grove, and the older guy all left early in the morning. They skipped breakfast and packed up their tents at record speed. They explained that they wanted to get over two passes that day—Mather Pass and Pinchot Pass.

I told them that I planned the same because I needed to meet my friend the following day. If I didn't do both passes, I wouldn't make it. I stopped earlier than I should have the night before; now I needed to make up for it.

Everyone took off, except for Trevor. He was slightly behind them. I could tell that he didn't think that I could make it over both passes in one day, especially if I hadn't left yet. I explained I wasn't going to skip breakfast, especially on a hard day.

I got packed up and was the last to leave camp. Trevor left about an hour before me, and Sam left 30 minutes before me. I left about 45 minutes earlier than I usually did, so I thought I was okay.

The trail was gray and rocky. The terrain didn't have any trees or bushes—just rocks. The mountain peaks surrounding me were steep gray rock as if they violently came up from the earth.

Climbing Mather Pass wasn't easy. Many of the rocks on the trail were loose rocks. They hurt my feet and took longer to get over.

When I arrived at the top of Mather Pass at 12,100 feet, I saw Sam and the two brothers. They were resting and eating a snack. The peak only had about 20 feet of flat area before it started down the other side. I joined the brothers and Sam and sat on a rock to eat a snack. I checked out the view but said I had to keep going if I was going to make it over two passes. I said goodbye and kept hiking.

I made my way down the mountain and had views for miles for most of the hike. I crossed rivers, climbed more rock stairs, and passed turquoise lakes. Some of

the crevasses in the mountains to my right still had snow packed inside because the sun didn't reach them.

One of the most incredible things about the JMT is you're often hiking between mountain ranges. The

mountains literally surround you. The sun gets blocked by early evening by the peaks, but then it makes areas glow as it sets.

At around mile eight to nine, I passed Sam (after leapfrogging a couple of times) and didn't run into her again for a few days.

After climbing up and down Mather Pass, I had to climb up Pinchot Pass. I had already climbed up 2,000 feet and down another 2,000 feet. Now I had an additional 2,000 feet up Pinchot. It was rocky, steep, and rugged. My feet were getting tired, and I had to refocus because my lazy feet would make me trip if I didn't.

One thing that kept me going was knowing that Trevor doubted me. There was something about him that made me feel competitive. My gut told me that he thought my ambitions were too high—like I wasn't an experienced hiker and had no right hiking the JMT.

I could see his shoe prints in the sand and dirt because they were very distinct prints. I knew he hadn't stopped yet and had made it over both passes. If he could, so could I. My stubbornness kept me going.

By the time I arrived at the top of Pinchot Pass at 12,050 feet, it was 6:25 pm. The top was rocky and colorless. I quickly enjoyed the views and faked a smile for a selfie.

Then, I started to hurry down the trail. I needed to find a place to camp, but it was too rocky and steep. I also needed a lake because I was almost out of water.

The landscape started to open up, and vegetation appeared. I hadn't seen a single person in several hours and started to feel nervous. When I finally found a lake, it was too far away, and there wasn't anywhere to camp.

I walked off the trail for a little bit because I saw an area that looked semi-flat. It didn't feel right, and I needed water. Finally, at 7:20 pm, I saw a lake to my right with trees surrounding it. I crossed the meadow and walked down to it. As I approached the water, I saw the older guy who was with the group. He said, "Hey! We're camped just up the hill! Come join us; there are other tent spaces."

I scooped up water and started walking up the hill, back towards the trail. Trevor had just set his tent up and was going to get water when he saw me. Surprised, he said, "Wow! We just got here like 20 minutes ago. We haven't even eaten dinner yet. Come join us."

I saw their three tents near each other, and I set mine up about 100 feet away, so I had some privacy. Once it was all set up, I made my dinner and took it to their campsite where they had a fire going. It was dark outside, and I used my bear can as a chair.

They asked if I had seen Sam, and I explained that I passed her around mile nine and hadn't seen her since. We assumed she set up camp somewhere else.

As we sat around eating, Trevor said, "Christy, I must admit, I underestimated you. I thought there was no way you'd make it this far today, especially after leaving later than us."

I knew it! I was happy that he confirmed what I suspected and glad that he now saw my potential.

Grove spoke up, "I had faith in you. I told them that

I wouldn't be surprised if you came rounding that corner, and then, there you were!"

That made me feel good that Grove knew that I was more capable than I appeared. I sometimes breathe like I'm dying, but I push through the pain. I don't stop, especially when I'm being stubborn or competitive.

I was grateful for Trevor underestimating me—it was exactly what I needed to push through the pain. I needed to prove to myself that I could do it. I am often motivated by people underestimating me.

I appreciated that Trevor told me he now saw my capabilities. Anytime someone can be honest about their thoughts and feelings, and then change their opinion once they gather more information, that's where great character lies.

I felt like part of the crew that night; a group of respected, experienced hikers. We all sat around telling stories and getting to know each other better.

> Camped around 11,000 feet
> Hiked 17 miles

Day

18

"You Look . . . Weathered"

I needed to get an earlier start than usual because this was the day that I needed to meet my friend Tori. I got up earlier and made my breakfast, and then started packing up. The others were eating their breakfast, and I told them that I was off to meet my friend. They planned to have an easy eight-mile day and enjoy Rae Lakes because the day before was so strenuous.

The group thought I was crazy and ambitious to hike 17–18 miles and climb up Glen Pass after going up two passes the day before. I explained that I made a commitment and I had no way of contacting my friend. If I didn't show, she'd wonder what happened to me.

I set off around 9:15 am and told myself that I could do it. It was a beautiful day with bright blue skies again. I wore my usual—shorts and a T-shirt.

I walked over rocks, followed the trail past waterfalls, and watched the leafy trees turn yellow. I tried to go fast, but I was also soaking up the beauty.

Then I arrived at a suspension bridge over a river. One thing I haven't mentioned is my fear of heights. I don't usually have issues when I feel stable, so mountain tops don't bother me. It's when I feel shaky and unstable that I freeze, sweat, and freak out. I can only go up two steps on a ladder because I feel like I'm going to fall. And I'm tall—that's a *hard* fall.

I climbed up the steps, and there was a wooden sign that said, "One person at a time on bridge." I gazed across the bridge, and it swayed slightly in the wind. I gulped.

There was nobody else around. What if I fell to my demise? Who would know? I looked around to see if there was another way to cross, but this was it.

I knew the longer I stared at the bridge, the more I'd convince myself not to cross it. I decided just to go. I grabbed both sides of the metal rope railing and started walking. It shook and swayed, and I talked to myself

out loud, "It's okay. Hundreds, no thousands of people cross this bridge every season. They inspect it. It's safe. Nobody has fallen. You're safe . . . Shoot, it is the end of the season . . . maybe it's not stable anymore. No, it's safe; you're fine. It's safe. You're fine."

I literally spoke those words the entire time until I made it across. Hopefully, nobody was listening in the woods. I don't encourage you to Google, "Suspension bridge collapse while hikers crossing," because it might terrify you. Thankfully I didn't Google that until after I hiked the JMT. Always go one at a time.

I continued hiking and ran into a guy in his 40s–50s. We were wearing the same shoes and backpack! I mean, I was wearing men's since they don't make my size in women's, but still—it was hilarious! We briefly hiked together until he took off. His name was Russ, and he was completing a four-day loop. When he found out that

I was hiking alone, he said he was impressed. He told me how he went to Burning Man and described what a great experience that was for him.

I arrived at Rae Lakes, and they were spectacular! I was so disappointed that I wasn't camping there. It consisted of a deep blue set of lakes surrounded by green trees, a yellow meadow, and mountains encasing the whole area!

Thankfully, the trail took me along the side of the lakes for about a mile and a half, so I got to enjoy them. It was one of the most beautiful places I've seen on the JMT.

I paused at a stream and debated if I should fill up on water because I seemed to be running lower than expected at that time—probably because it was warm out and I had already completed a lot of miles. I decided against it because it would take too long to filter the water.

I continued around the lakes, and at the end of them, Glen Pass began. There was a sign marking the start of the pass, and someone left a handwritten note for other members in their group. I thought that was a good idea and that maybe Tori and I could communicate with each other that way.

The path around Rae Lakes was fairly flat, and right after the sign, the trail immediately started to climb on steep switchbacks. It was already at least 4:00 pm, but I needed to continue. It was just under two miles, and almost 1,400 feet elevation gain to the top of the pass.

After about a quarter of a mile, I ran into a thin girl going down. I asked her how far the peak was, and she said, "You're trying to summit today?"

I sheepishly said, "Yeah." The girl said with an attitude, "Good luck," and continued past me.

Great. I continued climbing, and the trail turned into rock steps and then just rocks in an almost complete vertical way. When I looked up the path, the sun blinded me because the trail was pointing to the sky.

I was so exhausted and wondered why the pass was so difficult. Was it because I had a long day prior and had already hiked almost 14 miles before I started Glen Pass?

No, this was a crazy steep and rugged section! I huffed and puffed and said a lot of curse words. I got angry because it just wouldn't give me a break. I was so close to meeting Tori, but yet so, so far away.

I was approaching the top and noticed two guys eating a snack. In the distance, I saw a lake on the other side of the top. As I came to the guys, I asked, "Is this the top?" They laughed.

They pointed around the corner, and it was on a false peak! I screamed in pain and frustration while stomping my trekking poles into the ground.

The men looked at me like I was crazy. I said that I had a very hard few days, and I needed to make it over the pass to meet someone. They said it was another 500 feet and half a mile to the top.

I continued hiking and felt like crying. I was in a ton of pain, almost out of water, and the peak looked like it touched the sky. I had no choice—I had to continue. There wasn't anywhere to camp even if I wanted to.

That last 500 feet involved about 40 zigzag rock switchbacks. The sun was starting to set, and I thought I might pass out on the trail. It became sharp, jagged rocks on the narrow path that was hard to navigate. A father and son team were climbing down, and I asked how much farther. They said, "About 20 switchbacks." I sighed and kept going.

I did my best to remember all of those quotes that friends sent me in the letters. They were so proud of me. I was a beast. I was brave. I could do anything through Christ who strengthens me. Right?

They wanted to hear all about my adventure. I couldn't tell them how I stopped on the pass—how I gave up just a few miles from Tori. I pushed through the pain and forced myself to keep lifting my legs. Each step felt like a ton of effort and I focused on one step up at a time.

Finally, at 6:25 pm, I made it to the top at 11,926 feet! I was the only person at the peak, and the sun was disappearing. I took a selfie, but this time I was screaming in it. I decided no more fake smiles. I was angry and tired, and it was going to show.

The top consisted of the two-foot-wide trail going across the top section for about 30 feet, and that was it. The surrounding edges were sharp and monstrous.

I looked around on both sides of the pass and felt like I could see the entire world. The peaks in the distance looked like the tips of a meringue pie.

I earned that view. I *deserved* that view.

At the end of the season, there was a hiker survey for anyone who hiked the JMT, and the results showed that the hardest pass was voted as Glen Pass. I hiked that pass after a long two days, so I felt justified in being beaten up by that beast.

I quickly started to head down and knew it was another two miles to the Kearsarge Pass trail junction. I was officially out of water and probably dehydrated.

I couldn't believe how fast the sun was disappearing. The sun was still out but was blocked by mountains. I saw an incredible sunset of yellow illuminating the peaks, but it became darker and darker on the trail. I picked up the pace, and it was easier going downhill. I didn't want to spend the time to find my headlamp in the backpack,

and it was too time-consuming and painful to take the pack off and get it back on.

I focused on the trail and the rocks below the dirt. I intentionally kept my feet up to avoid tripping in the limited light. It was the darkest that I had ever hiked, but I was so close—I couldn't stop now! I thanked God for the almost full moon that night, which helped to keep the trail semi-visible.

After two miles, I arrived at the Kearsarge Pass sign. It was around 7:45 pm. I used the light on my camera to read the sign, and there was a note for me!

The note was written on a torn section of a permit and taped to the sign. It read, "Christy, We are at Charlotte Lake. Hope to see you there. We have the goods! Tori and Taylor."

I was so thrilled! They were close! I walked another 50 feet, and there was an opening with a flat section to my right and a trail leading down to Charlotte Lake. In the distance, I saw a headlamp. Then I heard, "Christy? Is that you?"

I shouted back, "Yes! It's me!!" I ran towards Tori's light as she ran towards me, and we hugged. I was so excited to see her and to know that I made it. All of my effort was worth it; I succeeded in my goal!

Tori shined her light on me and said, "You look . . ." She paused, trying to figure out how to say what she was thinking. She continued, ". . . *weathered*. Are you okay?"

I explained that I was out of water and really needed to filter water at the lake. Tori explained that Charlotte Lake was at least a mile and a half away and 400 feet down. She gave me some of her water to drink, but I didn't have enough to make dinner. That was okay because they brought me granola bars and snacks!

Tori introduced me to her friend, Taylor. They had met recently through a mutual friend. Tori was about 25 years old, had long blonde hair, and was around 6' tall. Taylor was around the same age and had long brown hair. They were both fit, healthy, and beautiful.

Tori brought me to a large rock where she dumped out her bear can filled with snacks and food for me to eat whatever I wanted. Then she showed me a piece of chocolate cake that she brought for me! I almost cried and started eating the cake right away. She reached out to my sister to find out which type of treat I'd like, which was so thoughtful.

Then Tori showed me the massive bottle of whiskey that she brought. We each took a shot and talked about our experiences. They had driven up Friday night after work and slept in Tori's huge SUV because she realized it would be easier than setting up their tent. They had views of the stars through the sunroof.

That morning, they hiked about seven miles on Kearsarge Pass Trail, and they said it was one of the most beautiful trails they had ever hiked. Tori and Taylor arrived in the afternoon and hiked down to Charlotte Lake, but when I hadn't shown up, they realized it would be better to set up a tent in the area near the trail so I wouldn't miss them.

Tori said that Charlotte Lake was breathtaking and recommended that I hike there in the morning. I explained that I would have to go down there to get water for my breakfast, so I'd have to take the side trip.

I was so full of joy knowing these women hiked in to see me and bring me goodies. I told them how hard it was to get over Glen Pass but that I had told everyone I would make it by the 17th to meet her, and I was determined to do so.

Tori told me that I was her hero, and I felt so proud to have their support and encouragement. She said that Barry, our coworker who told me about the trail, kept asking if I was okay and alive, and she'd have to report back to him.

After an hour of catching up and eating snacks, Tori and Taylor said it was too cold, and they needed to get inside the tent. They were sharing a two-person tent, and I set mine up next to theirs. I took some ibuprofen and laid down in my thermals.

I made it. I had 45 miles left to go and four full days

to do it. I could relax. I hiked 75 miles in five days over several mountain passes to be there, in that moment. I felt like I could do anything.

➤ Camped at 10,750 feet
➤ Hiked 18 miles

19

Cake and Whiskey

At 6:30 am, Tori and Taylor were squirming around in their tent. I was awake too. Tori asked, "Christy, did you know you were coughing all night?" I responded, "Yep. I've developed a cough because it's warm during the day and cold at night."

Tori and Taylor said they were so cold; they were going to skip breakfast and pack up so they could start warming up while hiking. They also knew that the sun would come out soon and wanted to position themselves directly in it.

We all got out of our tents, and they packed up quickly. Tori was shivering and asked me, "How are you doing this night after night for three weeks?!"

I said, "Tori, there are cold nights on the JMT, and there are *freezing* nights on the JMT."

Tori asked, "What was last night?"

I explained, "Last night was just cold. There's no frost on our tents."

Tori gasped and said she was freezing. She said,

"Well, you look better this morning. Last night I was worried about you. You looked really weathered. Your cheeks were sunken in and everything."

I hadn't seen myself in a mirror for days, so I had no idea how I looked, but I can imagine after those insane five days, I must have looked weathered.

As soon as they were packed up, they took off, hiking back to their car seven miles away.

I needed water and started walking down the trail to Charlotte Lake, wearing my long-sleeve shirt and pants (with thermals underneath). I felt like I was a mess; my hair wasn't even pulled back. For the first time, I left my backpack inside the tent while I took my expensive watch, camera, and phone with me. I figured people would think someone was inside sleeping and wouldn't bother my stuff.

I also carried that large, heavy, glass bottle of whiskey. I told Tori that there was no way that I could hike with that heavy thing, and she didn't want to carry the weight on her way back either. According to the map, there were bear boxes in places around the lake. You're not supposed to leave food in there, but I figured someone would want the whiskey, a ranger if no one else.

It took longer than I expected, and I searched for a bear box. I found one and left the whiskey inside, so at least the animals couldn't get to it. Then I had to walk halfway around the lake to find a spot where I could get water.

There was a flat rock that almost acted as a dock, and I quickly scooped up water. As soon as I had 15 ounces filtered, I poured it into my water bottle and drank it nonstop. I have never been as thirsty as I was then. I must have consumed 40 ounces of water while sitting on that rock filtering more water.

The lake was absolutely incredible! It was surrounded by rolling hills thick with pine trees. Directly across from me was a steep mountain peak. The trees and mountains reflected in the still water. There wasn't anybody around, and I sat there soaking up the sun and views. I felt fulfilled. I didn't have to rush; I was actually a little ahead of schedule.

Once I filled up my water bottle and four-liter filter, I climbed back up the mountain. I was starting to sweat because of the heat and because I had on long layers. By the time I arrived back at my tent, the sun was on full display.

I made my oatmeal and latte and then decided to top it off with the second half of the chocolate cake that Tori brought me. I mean, it would melt otherwise—I was just being responsible. I put my shorts on and sat on a rock while I savored it.

Just then, a couple came hiking up from the lake. They stopped to chat and wanted to know if I found my friend. Tori and Taylor met them the day before, so I happily told them that I was able to connect with them, but they hurried away because of the cold.

The couple was hiking a loop over a few days. They commented about my chocolate cake, and I exclaimed, "My friends brought it to me!" They stared at it in jealousy. The only problem was now I had to put the plastic container from the store in my bear can to hike it out.

I didn't leave my campsite until 11:40 am, but I only planned on hiking eight miles that day. It was hot outside, and my left foot was throbbing. Now that I could slow down, I realized that my foot was very sore. It felt like it had been twisted.

The views that appeared in the clearings were breathtaking. The mountain peaks were higher and even more spectacular. The valleys below were speckled in green and yellow as a sign of the changing season.

Sometimes the trail was only about a foot wide, and other times it stretched to two feet. Often the trail cuts through brush or a meadow. I hiked slower, enjoying the scenery and blue sky.

Right after I started hiking for the day, I saw those identical shoe prints that matched Trevor's soles. I was shocked and frustrated. *Had they passed me while I was*

at Charlotte Lake getting water? No, that couldn't be. They would have had to climb up Glen Pass all before 11:40 am.

Even though it was unlikely that they had done that, those shoe prints haunted me. I wanted all of my hard work the last two days to pay off and at least have a bit of a lead. If they passed me, maybe Glen Pass wasn't as hard as I thought?

I know hiking isn't a competition. It's just that I'm a competitive person, and being ahead of someone who thought he was a better hiker than me gave me satisfaction. Now I wasn't sure if there was someone out there with the identical shoe or if it was Trevor. I ran into a man with the exact same shoe as me, so there might have been someone else with Trevor's shoes.

It was now September 17th, towards the end of the season. Each day I saw fewer people, especially northbound. It was way too late in the season for someone to start hiking northbound because they'd run into snow at the passes before they could finish. Those of us hiking southbound were now hiking at different paces.

I've heard some people say that the JMT is a highway. That might be true during other months, but I wouldn't classify it as a highway. I saw the most people in Yosemite Valley for the first 30 miles because people were doing day hikes. Once I got past Tuolumne Meadows, there were significantly fewer people. I often camped near places where I saw other tents, but they were in the distance and not intruding on my space by any means. It gave me a sense of comfort knowing another human was in the area.

About halfway into my day, the terrain turned into rocks again. I hadn't planned on going over Forester Pass that day, and I didn't feel that well. My stomach hurt, and I had gas pains. Perhaps that cake wasn't the best idea. I also felt dizzy at times, which might have been the elevation or because I was still on my period.

One strange thing that happened on the JMT was the urgency to go pee. I wouldn't feel the need for hours, and then once I stopped for a snack or realized I needed to go, it was like my body screamed, "Now!" I had to find a hidden place and take my pack off. I used toilet paper that I packed out, so I had to grab that too. But several times, I almost peed myself because once my body knew I was stopping, it wanted to go right then and there. I should have made more frequent stops, but I didn't realize I needed to go.

I kept walking because I get bored easily and figured I had to get the miles in at some point; it might as well be then.

The trail on Forester Pass was long and diagonal on the side of the mountain. It was the longest switchback that I experienced. I guess it wasn't really a switchback, it felt like walking up a never-ending ramp. The higher I went, the more it looked like I was on the moon with no life in sight.

The last section before the peak was steep, and I could see a lake below. The sun lit up the mountains in beautiful ways as it started to descend. The mountains were now shadows on other peaks.

I reached the 13,200-foot peak at 6:45 pm, the latest that I had been on a peak. I was all alone and hadn't seen another human in many hours. I stood there looking out in all directions. It was a vast wilderness, and I was at one of the highest points.

The most satisfying thing about standing at a peak is looking into the distance and knowing you were miles and miles away earlier in the day. I would try to find where I started the day, but it was always too far away to

see. It was astonishing to see how far I hiked that day. There were no roads in sight, no buildings, and no disruption to nature.

I felt accomplished on the peaks. I earned every single view. Nobody could drive there; my feet took me there. I looked at the scenery that only a tiny fraction of people get to see with their own eyes. I felt incredibly blessed.

I started to climb down, knowing that I needed to stop soon to camp before it was too dark. After about a mile (at 7:00 pm), I found a small lake in a sea of rocks and then found a small section near the trail that was flat and where I could set up my tent.

It was eerie—complete silence. The lake was perfectly still, and the only vegetation was small patches of grasses between some rocks. Once I got my water and set my tent up, I used my trekking pole and balanced it between some rocks so it was sticking up. Then I hung my light from the pole so that I could see my dinner cooking.

It was dark outside, and I laughed that I was always eating in the dark. The dark started to creep me out a little, but I reminded myself of what it looked like in the light. I told myself that it wasn't scary; it was just desolate.

I climbed inside my tent and hung my light from a loop at the top of my tent. As I laid down, I noticed a massive daddy-long-leg next to me. I quickly sat up and then noticed that one was inside my tent and another one was on the outside. I unzipped the mesh door and grabbed a tissue to throw the guy out. I looked around and made sure there weren't other bugs inside. It was the only time that I had insects inside my tent (other than the wasp on day one).

The moon was bright with no trees to block it. Being at 13,000 feet, I felt like I was in space. I had a hard time sleeping because the moon created so much light shining through my tent—nature's nightlight.

➤ Camped at 13,000 feet
➤ Hiked 13 miles

Day

20

Reflection

I had to go to the bathroom when I woke up, and I looked around to find a hidden place. No such luck as most rocks weren't big enough. I found one that would cover me from at least one side of the trail, and I figured nobody would be hiking over the pass yet.

I made my breakfast and looked around at the still,

quiet landscape. I made it through being completely alone almost the entire day and night.

As I packed up my stuff, an older man from India came hiking up the trail. My tent was only a few feet from the trail, so he stopped to talk to me.

He was wild and eccentric. The man told me how he'd hiked the JMT many times. Then he pulled out a joint and started smoking it. I was shocked—it wasn't even 10:00 am. The man asked me if I wanted some, and I declined. He started talking about psychedelics and how they open your mind. As he spoke, he kept asking if I wanted some drugs. I kept declining and was feeling a little uncomfortable. There was nobody else in sight. I continued to pack up, trying to give a hint. Eventually, the man continued hiking northbound.

I continued my trip to the south. The trail was a straight path through rocks as it slowly descended the mountain. As I got lower, more vegetation appeared.

It was a wide-open landscape with wide-spread views in front of me. Once I made it through the open area, I started climbing up a mountain and through trees.

This back and forth between hilly, tree-filled mountains to flatter desert areas with wide-open views continued several times. Back and forth. This section was easier because the trail only slowly descended, and I had a view in front of me the whole time. It was different from most of the JMT.

I still climbed up mountains and crossed rivers, and I realized that my time on the JMT ended soon. There was a sadness knowing that my grand adventure was almost over. It had gone by so fast, yet I couldn't wait to shower or to sleep in a bed.

I had been in the wilderness for almost three weeks, and yet I still didn't have any answers about my marriage. There wasn't a sudden clarity or decision. I was still stuck and undecided.

However, I had learned that I could live on my own. I didn't need my husband; now the question was, did I want him? He hadn't even mailed a letter to me. I didn't want to believe that he'd be so cold; he kept saying he didn't want to be separated. I tried to rationalize that he probably sent it late and it would be forwarded to my home address.

I realized that I hadn't thought about my husband as much as I should have. I enjoyed meeting new people and having new adventures so much that he was on the backburner. That wasn't a good feeling. I didn't miss him. I felt more like myself without him.

I thought about what it would have been like if my

husband were on the trail with me, and I didn't like what I envisioned. We wouldn't have had as good of conversations that I had getting to know new people. He would have made me make all of the decisions. He wouldn't have loved the outdoors like I do. He would have gone to please me, but he wouldn't have enjoyed it.

I listened to music, reflected, and asked God for help. I prayed and thanked God for the opportunity that he provided, for keeping me safe, and for giving me the strength to carry on. Now I needed help with my life outside of the trail.

I asked God to show me what was right—to tell me what to do. I pleaded with Him for guidance. Being in nature, surrounded by God's creation, is the perfect opportunity to spend time with God.

Deep in my gut, I knew my marriage was over ten months earlier when my husband lied while in Atlanta, but I couldn't get myself to be okay with losing my marriage. I was 36 and didn't want to start over. We had built a life together. I still wanted kids at some point, but it never felt right to have them with him. I knew the odds of finding someone else and having kids at that age were unlikely. It takes time to find a partner.

I wasn't just giving up a decade-long marriage; I was giving up the likelihood of having children. I would be giving up my in-laws, who were the only family I had in California. I would lose 12 people if I lost my husband. Was I prepared to be alone without a local family? Most of his family stopped talking to me when I asked him to move out. Maybe they never considered me family, after all.

I thought about all of this while praying, listening to music, and soaking up the wilderness. People often asked me what I listened to on my iPod Shuffle, and it was a huge mix. I put the iPod on shuffle because I like variety. I had alternative, slow songs, hip-hop, rock, and Christian music.

Here are a few of the artists that were on my playlist:

- Carly Rae Jepsen (the entire Emotion album)
- Shawn Mendes—Life of the Party
- The Lumineers—Ophelia
- Flo Rida—My House
- Empire of the Sun—Alive
- Mike Posner—I Took a Pill in Ibiza
- Cold War Kids—First
- Charli XCX—Boom Clap
- Parade of Lights—We're the Kids
- Gorillaz—Stylo
- Timbaland—Give It a Go
- Grouplove—Tongue Tied
- MercyMe—Bring the Rain
- The Temper Trap—Sweet Disposition
- Francesca Battistelli—Free to Be Me; It's Your Life
- Guns N' Roses—Welcome to the Jungle
- The Chainsmokers—Closer
- For King & Country—Priceless

It might look like a strange mix, but it got me through each mood and each climb. Music enhances my ability to think and experience emotions. Some people listen to audiobooks, which is totally fine for them, but I prefer music.

Another thing that I frequently thought about is the difference between hiking the trail in 2016 vs. hiking it 100 or 500 years earlier. I was extremely fortunate to have lightweight, state-of-the-art equipment. I had a down-feathered coat and sleeping bag, a Jetboil, and a small can of gas to cook my food. I had a filter to clean my water. I can't imagine what it was like for people ages ago trekking through those lands—what an incredible time for us to be alive.

As I continued hiking, I covered more ground than I anticipated because it was a more leisurely day, going slightly downhill for a few miles.

I was getting closer to Mount Whitney, and in the distance, dark blue storm clouds appeared. They appeared out of nowhere and circled Whitney. I heard the afternoons have a tendency to create storms, and I was witnessing it with my own eyes.

I passed the sign for Crabtree and realized that I wasn't that far from Guitar Lake, just a few miles, so I kept going. When I was halfway up a mountain, I ran into two men who had a camp set up about 60 feet off the trail. They had music playing on a speaker, and their shirts were off.

I stopped, and the men approached me, asking where I was headed and how my hike was. I got a feeling that they were "bros," and something felt off about them. I didn't care for blasting music on a speaker in nature, and they looked like meatheads in their late 30s. They offered to let me stay there, but I kept hiking instead.

When I reached the peak just before Guitar Lake, the sun was setting, creating an incredible yellow glow and illuminating the mountains.

I climbed down and arrived at Guitar Lake. I saw a man in his 30s, with a tent set up at the beginning of the lake. I found a spot about 100 feet from him and a little farther from the lake. I set up my tent and walked to get water.

I ran into the man, and we talked about the fact that there were only a few people there. I had read that Guitar Lake is overcrowded because it's the closest water source to Mount Whitney from the north side. We looked across the lake, and there were a few tents high up on some rocks, but that was it.

The man said he already talked to that group, and they were planning to start hiking Mount Whitney at 2:00 am so they could see the sunrise. I told the man that I had no intention of hiking the tallest peak in the contiguous U.S. in the dark. He agreed and said he planned to take it easy the following day, hanging out at the lake. Then in the afternoon, he'd hike up and watch the sunset.

I was always on passes at sunset, so it felt appropriate to do the same with Whitney. I wasn't in a hurry—I had two days to complete Whitney and to hike back down the Whitney portal. I also had a few extra days that I could use if I were to fall behind. However, my OCD kicked in, and I really wanted to finish in three weeks. If I finished in two days, it would put me at 22 days on the trail, but two of the days would be half days.

I told the guy that I'd probably do the same.

I made my dinner and stared up at Whitney. There it was, just above me. It was a massive rock with sharp edges until it reached the sky. I thought, *Tomorrow, I'll be at the top.*

➤ Camped at 11,400 feet
➤ Hiked 18 miles

Day

21

Just Me and Whitney

When I woke up, I noticed that the other tents farther up the trail were gone. It was just the guy next to me and me. The sun came out, and I made my breakfast. I wasn't in a hurry and was still trying to decide when to summit the nearby beast.

Suddenly, the two men I had met on the trail before arriving at Guitar Lake showed up. They were meeting their friend, the guy who was closer to the lake. They said hello and then met their friend. Within minutes, they had their shirts off again, making a ruckus.

The men walked over to me and said they were going to lounge around the lake and hike up half of Whitney in the afternoon. They explained that there is a small area on the mountainside where only three tents would fit. You have to carry extra water because there is no water source nearby. They were going to set up their tents and then climb the last two miles to the peak to watch the sunset, then climb down back to their tent for the night.

They said that I could join them and put my tent on the shelf with them. I said I'd think about it.

I tried to repack my bear can and prepare my food for the day, and a little chipmunk would not leave me alone. He was cute, but he was trying to steal my food. He got inches from me and my food, and I even tried to scare him away, but he didn't have it. Suddenly, three chipmunks were trying to get my food.

I sat there enjoying the view but started to feel bored. The area was just rocks and the lake, which became drab after a while. There was something off about those guys, and I didn't feel comfortable around them. Out of my entire three weeks on the trail, they were the only ones who made me feel uncomfortable. I started packing up to leave, and when I went to put my electrolyte stick in my water bottle, I couldn't find it.

I walked over to the guys all packed up and explained that I was going to start hiking Mount Whitney. They said they'd save me a spot at the cliff area just in case. I mentioned something about my electrolyte stick missing, and they laughed, saying they saw a chipmunk running with a black and green stick, and they wondered what it was. That little thief stole it!

I started hiking Mount Whitney, and the climb was steep from the beginning. I was alone, and I took micro-breaks to catch my breath. The trail was only a foot wide at times; others, it got up to two feet. I put my pants and jacket on as the chilly air started setting in.

I was hiking slowly because of the elevation and difficulty when suddenly, the men almost caught up to me. I hurried along and passed the shelf where three tents could fit. I made it to the junction where the final trail to the top splits off.

I read that JMT hikers leave their packs at the junction and only take their lid with some food and water to the top. It was two miles to the peak from there, and it became steep and dangerous. Hiking with a huge, heavy pack wasn't ideal. The PCT cuts off at Crabtree, and Whitney isn't part of their trail, so it's mostly JMT hikers and people hiking it in a day or two days.

I saw a few large backpacks sitting on the small area, and I took mine off too. Unfortunately, this signaled to my body that it wanted to pee. I had nowhere to go, but I found a small spot on the edge where the men couldn't see me as well.

Then I saw a colossal marmot trying to get into someone's backpack. I read that the animals can unzip bags because they have thumbs. I tried to scare him away with my trekking pole, and he wouldn't budge. I even tapped him with it. Eventually, I got him off the packs.

I got my backpack lid ready and strapped it around my waist to take just that with some snacks and water to the top. As I was getting it ready, one of the guys walked over to me from their ledge where they were setting up. It was about 100 feet below me. He asked me, "You're going to the summit now?" I replied, "Yeah. I might as well. I'm so close."

The man told me that they'd save me a spot if I wanted to camp with them. Then I began climbing up. The clouds were starting to circle the peak just like the day before, but they weren't dark, just white.

It felt good not to have that heavy backpack weighing

me down. The trail became narrow and steep, and I had to focus on where to put my feet.

As I climbed up, about ten different people passed me, going downhill. Each minute, it got darker, colder, and foggier. I was wearing my pants over my spandex shorts, a sports bra and T-shirt, and my puffy blue coat. I put my gloves on and was also wearing my baseball hat. I was grateful that I had my headband that also covered my ears.

The people I passed were in a hurry because of the weather, and it was already 4:00 pm. Many were in shorts. I got nervous because I was the only person hiking up; everyone else was headed down.

I briefly talked with a man in his 50s as he was going down and asked how much farther. He said, "You're so close. Don't worry about the weather; you'll get there soon." He could see the look of panic on my face.

I explained that I was worried about my backpack being torn apart by marmots, and he said, "When I get back there, I'll put rocks on it to keep it safe. What does it look like?" I described my backpack, and he continued climbing down.

The trail wasn't really a trail; it was more like climbing on jagged rocks on the side of the mountain. At one point, I looked down through a crevasse, and it was a straight fall down on rocks. The rocks were almost vertical like God smashed them together until they rose from the earth.

I was one mile from the top when it started to snow. I couldn't believe it. I wondered if I should keep going and

decided that I couldn't give up so close to the finish. I kept going, reminding myself that I experienced a hail storm halfway through and survived. Then I started to worry about the lightning that accompanied the last storm.

I kept climbing anyway. The snow was just a flurry, and it wasn't sticking. But the clouds were starting to close in tighter.

Then I reached the peak! It was a large section of flat rocks almost stacked together. I saw a building in

the distance and walked towards it. It was closed off and locked, but it looked neat up there. It was a stone building sitting on the rocks. There were piles of rock slabs, and I walked around.

I was the only person up there! I marveled at making it to the top and the official end to the John Muir Trail.

I looked around and saw 360-degree views. I was the queen of the castle! Everything was below me. The clouds encompassed the entire area, but they were higher than the mountain peaks. I saw the mountains in all directions, then a layer of sky, and above that, the layer of clouds sat above them. It was almost like the clouds weren't allowed to go lower. Not yet anyway.

I wanted to eat something because I hadn't eaten lunch, but I was nervous that I was there alone. Was I the only person crazy enough to be at the top during an incoming storm?

There was a sign at the top that stated:

EXTREME DANGER FROM LIGHTNING

To avoid being struck by lightning, immediately leave
the area if any of the following conditions apply.

- Dark Clouds nearby
- Thunder, Hail, or Rain
- Hissing in the Air
- Static Electricity in the Hair or Fingertips

THE WHITNEY SHELTER WILL NOT OFFER
PROTECTION. YOU SHOULD LEAVE THE SUMMIT
AND PROCEED TO A LOWER ELEVATION.

I didn't feel static or see lightning, but I know it changes rapidly at that elevation. I thought that I should probably leave—I was indeed the only crazy person at the top.

I read another sign that said:

National Park Service U.S. Department of the Interior

Mount Whitney elevation 14,496.811 feet
John Muir Trail—High Sierra Trail
September 5th, 1930

This tablet marks the construction of the
highest trail in the United States. Begun in
1928. It was completed in 1930 under the
direction of the National Park Service working
with the United States Forest Service.

Suddenly, I heard people. I followed their voice, and someone popped up from the rock cliff! I peeked over the edge and saw rock climbers climbing to the top!

I was blown away! About eight people climbed up. I said, "Wow! You rock-climbed up here?" One guy said, "You hiked up it!"

I felt better about not being alone, so I took some time to take photos and videos. Then I sat down and ate some snacks.

I talked with a few of the rock climbers and found out they were from Pasadena, California. Three women and a man were nurses, and all worked together. They had been preparing for the climb for months. I told them that I just completed the entire JMT—211 miles (plus some extra).

The rock climbers took a few pictures of me, and I stretched my arms out to the sky. I felt accomplished and proud. I couldn't believe that I actually did it!

I looked around, and the clouds were white in one direction and dark blue in another. I could even see rain streaming from the blue clouds in the distance. I was just so grateful that I still had views before the clouds took over.

I spent about 30 minutes at the top, and then the clouds engulfed the area, and the snow increased. It was almost like hail because it was perfectly round white balls of hard-packed snow.

I started to head down, and the rocks were now wet and the little round pebbles of snow/hail were all over the ground. I put my gloves on and searched in my lid for that last remaining heat packet. I opened it and put a square in each glove. I was satisfied that I chose to use the two packages I picked up at Red's Meadow on the two days that it snowed and hailed.

I was so happy—I had completed the uphill climbs. It would be all downhill from there!

When I was about a mile from the top, I ran into the group of four hiking up! Sam, Trevor, Grove, and Mike had smiles on their faces. Trevor and Sam were in pants, coats, gloves, and hats. Grove and Mike were wearing shorts and coats. I suddenly realized those weren't Trevor's shoe tracks—I was still ahead of them!

When they saw me, they immediately asked, "Did you make it to Kearsarge Pass to meet your friend!?"

I exclaimed, "Yes!! And she brought me cake!"

In unison, they shouted, "Cake!!"

I was so thrilled to see them, but the weather was getting worse by the minute, and we were standing on the edge of a mountain. I took their picture in case I

didn't see them again, and then we carefully passed each other.

I continued hiking down, and it was harder navigating the edge with gravity wanting to pull me down. At one point, there was a two-foot, sharp, sloped rock that was entirely wet. I had no choice but to slide down it and prayed that I stopped at the bottom and didn't go off the edge to my demise.

I made it and felt relieved. I was in the clouds and couldn't see far away, making it an eerie trek.

I got closer to the junction and saw three tents where the guys set up on the edge. It was below me, but I could see the tents. It looked like three guys I had seen on and off (and only talked to briefly) had joined them.

When I arrived at the junction, I smiled when I saw three medium-sized rocks on the top, front, and side of my pack. The man put them there to ensure the marmots didn't attack. I love trail people.

Unfortunately, I didn't realize it would snow, and I didn't put my rain cover on. My backpack was wet but not soaking.

I put my backpack on, and it felt like it weighed 100 pounds! I struggled to get it on and almost fell over from the weight. I had just hiked four miles with only the lid and didn't realize what a difference that heavy pack made.

I started hiking south, and after a few feet, I was in for a surprise. I was still at the top of a ridge, and the trail started climbing another peak. I almost screamed. My backpack was so heavy, and I had mentally prepared for no more climbing! I felt robbed. Where was my downhill?

I don't know how far I had to climb up, but it felt like half a mile. Finally, the trail started to climb down the south side.

It was cloudy, and about half an inch of snow was

now formed on the trail. I made the first footprints in the snow.

At one point, there were metal poles on the edge with a metal handrail. The area was sloped, and the railing was necessary because there was a 20-foot long slab of ice on the trail. It wasn't just from the snow that day, there was a frozen waterfall on the rocks, and the water continued on the trail. It all had frozen. I slid across it and grabbed the handrail.

As I descended, the clouds cleared up in spots in the distance, and the snow stopped as it started to warm up a little.

After hiking five miles and almost 3,000 feet from the peak of Mount Whitney, I arrived at the first water source, a small lake at Trail Camp. There were already several tents from two-day hikers set up on the limited flat spaces. I was exhausted and found a spot.

It started to sprinkle, so I set up my tent quickly. As soon as it was up, it started raining much harder. I grabbed my bear can and put it 20–30 feet away. Then I jumped inside my tent. The rain came pouring down, and I was happy that I was in a shelter. I couldn't eat dinner in my tent, so I made a protein shake because it was still in my backpack for the day.

The rain pounded on my tent, and I recorded a video on my camera, Blair Witch-style, about how exhausted I was and how the rain was pelting my tent. I hoped that my tent would stand up to the storm.

It was only 7:00 pm, but I had no choice but to try and sleep. The two guys close to me were snoring, and I grumbled. I cannot sleep near snorers, and the sound drives me insane. I put my headphones on and played music to try and block it out. I wrote a little bit but was too exhausted for much.

I laid there listening to my music and trying to soak up the last night in my tent. I had mixed feelings. I was sad that it was all over. I was so proud of my accomplishment. I couldn't wait to eat real food, take a shower, and sleep on a bed.

I had a hard time sleeping that night because I had to keep my headphones in with music playing, and they hurt my ears. It rained most of the night.

➤ Camped at 11,680 feet
➤ Hiked 10 miles

22

Legit Hiker

I woke up early and heard people packing up and leaving. Judging by my urgency to poop first thing in the morning throughout the past three weeks, I was worried. Where was I going to go? There were primarily rocks and not too many places that weren't visible from campsites or the trail. I stayed inside my tent until my neighbors were gone.

Mount Whitney has a rule about pooping—you have to use a WAG bag. The park ranger gave me a bag when I picked up my permit, and I carried it with me the entire time. You must poop inside the bag and carry it out with you. There are too many people hiking the mountain and not enough places to bury the poop. Typically, we're required to bury poop six inches deep and cover it back up. The peak was all rocks, so there was no burying it.

I dreaded the thought of pooping into a bag. I didn't have confidence that I could do it successfully, and then I'd have to carry it out? Not to mention how hard it was to squat at my age and height, with sore muscles and arthritic knees.

I climbed around the rocks and found a place. I was so relieved when all I had to do was pee! I think my mind made sure that my body was going to hold it.

I went to pack up my tent, and there was frost covering a quarter of my tent. The rain froze overnight; it was another freezing night on the JMT.

I didn't need to wait for my tent to thaw or dry out—I was hiking out of there! I wasn't going to sleep in my tent that night, so who cared if it was wet? Sure, it was heavier, but I was excited to reach the end.

I started hiking down, and it was nonstop descent—almost 3,500 feet in about seven miles.

I felt light and fresh. Excitement filled me—this was it! The last section! I made it!

Suddenly, I realized the trail got dicey and wild. Then I noticed I wasn't on Mount Whitney Trail. Crap. In my excitement, I had gotten off course somehow and was in a strange section of a lower rock peninsula.

I thought to myself, *Great; now you get lost?!*

I struggled to find the path and then saw two other people who were about to make my same mistake. I told them not to go that way, and we found where the trail continued. They took off, and I continued on my own.

I soaked up the mountains, trees, and the blue sky. I talked to the wilderness, "Thank you mountains. I love you trees. Goodbye bushes. I love you all."

I felt like I was skipping down the mountain, passing rivers as I descended lower and lower into the canyon.

All of a sudden, I ran into Grove and Mike! They said Trevor and Sam were just up ahead. They had all stayed at the same lake as me, but by the time they arrived, it was raining, and they had to set up in the dark and rain. They also said that by the time they arrived at the peak of Mount Whitney, it was a whiteout with clouds, and they couldn't see the views.

I think they passed me when I got lost on the trail. It was perfect that we were finishing the last two miles together.

Grove told me, "Christy, you were the topic of conversation the entire day that we hiked Glen Pass. We kept wondering how you hiked over Glen Pass after such a long day. It was challenging for us, and we *started* the day with Glen Pass! You are a legit hiker. Don't doubt yourself. You did more than most people can do."

I was beaming with pride and joy. Hearing that from such an experienced backpacker made me feel honored.

We arrived at a sign that said John Muir Wilderness, and Grove took my picture with it. We were less than a quarter-mile from the finish when we caught up with Trevor, Sam, and another guy that they had hiked with on and off.

The five of us crossed the finish together and were officially done with the JMT (and an extra 11 miles down Whitney Portal).

We had someone take a picture of the five of us (Sam, Jeff, Trevor, Christy, Grove, Mike), and I was so happy that I met them. They all kept me going. Trevor helped me to push harder and faster, *just* when I needed that push. Grove's encouragement helped me see my capabilities. Sam's friendship provided me with comfort, knowing she was also a solo female adventurer. The deadline to meet Tori ensured I didn't give up.

There was a parking lot and a small restaurant and shop at the trailhead. I bought a bacon burger with fries and a Pepsi. We all sat outside at a table together. The food was mouth-watering! It was early afternoon, and the

sun was shining. It was much warmer than at the top of
Whitney.

We reminisced about our time on the trail and
described how much we were looking forward to showers and beds.

I used the outdoor toilet and then walked over to the
group in a section where we could try to hitchhike back
to Lone Pine. It was 11 miles down the mountain on a
paved road. My car was at the golf course, but the others
needed to get to their motels.

There was construction going on, so traffic was
stopped for ten minutes at a time. We asked the cars
who were lined up, waiting to get past the construction,
for a ride. The problem is that there were a lot of us, and
we had massive packs.

I walked up to a jeep Cherokee or something similar,
and, when they rolled down their window, I saw that it
was the nurses who rock-climbed up Mount Whitney! I
asked for a ride, and they only had space for one. I'd have
to put my backpack in front of me.

I told the group that I'd get my car once I got to the
bottom and drive back up to give them a ride to Lone
Pine. I hopped in the car, and it took about 45 minutes to
get to the town because of the construction wait times. I
talked with the nurses and their experience climbing and
told them about my adventure.

They dropped me off at my car, and I drove back
up to Whitney Portal. I picked up Sam, Trevor, Grove,
and Mike and took them to where they requested to be
dropped off. We said our goodbyes and exchanged contact information.

I started driving out of the small town when I saw three hitchhikers outside of the McDonald's. I recognized them as the three guys who I had leapfrogged a few times. We had brief conversations, and they passed me just before we all finished.

I wanted to stop, but I had already passed them. My gut told me to go back, and I fought it. I didn't want to turn around; I wanted a Slurpee. But they were fellow backpackers. I needed to turn around.

I went back and pulled over in front of the hitchhikers. I rolled down the passenger window, and when they peeked their heads inside, they said, "Hey! It's you!" I responded, "It's you!"

We hadn't gotten each other's names. They were the three guys who joined the other three guys on the ridge of Whitney to camp. They told me that all three of them squeezed inside one tent because there wasn't much room on that ledge.

I asked where they were going, and they said, "As far south as you'll take us." I said, "Yes, but where are you trying to get?"

The guys looked defeated and said, "Los Angeles."

I exclaimed, "I'm going to Los Angeles!"

The guys were super excited. I asked them where in LA they needed to get—it is a big area, after all. They said Laguna Beach, and I said, "Well, that's south Orange County, so I'll tell you what—I'll take you to Lakewood where I live. It's on the border of Orange County. You can take an Uber from there, and it will cost around $35. Split the cost, and it'll be about $10 each."

I got out and opened the trunk, but it would only

fit two more packs with my backpack. One guy sat up front, while two guys sat in the back with a backpack in between them. We all squeezed into my Nissan Altima.

Before I took off, I said, "I have a knife (my pocket knife), and if anyone tries anything, I'll stab you." They laughed awkwardly.

We took off, and it was already close to 5:00 pm. I told the guys that I had been craving a Mountain Dew Slurpee, and as soon as I saw a gas station, I was going to stop. They laughed at my high school taste in drinks. I don't know what it was, maybe it was the heat, but I really wanted that ice-cold Slurpee.

Unfortunately, we were quickly out of town, and it took at least an hour before we came to a gas station. I used the restroom, and when I came out, the guys said, "We're sorry, but they don't have a Slurpee machine." They were so sweet and told me that the gas station did sell Mountain Dew. I bought a regular one and a Code Red. I rarely drink soda, but I was really craving it. We were in heaven. We all bought a few snacks and hit the road.

It was a four-hour drive to Lakewood, and we got to know each other. They were Taylor, Travis, and Nick. Taylor and Travis were brothers. They were all aged 23–25. The guys were from Boulder, Colorado, and hiked the entire JMT. They were trying to get to Orange County, where the brothers had an uncle.

They called their uncle and excitedly told him that they found a ride and would be there around 9:30 pm. Their uncle said he'd have lasagna waiting for them. They were all so ecstatic. They explained that they looked into a rental car from Lone Pine, and there weren't any available. It's a small town, and they were all booked.

The guys checked with U-Haul to see if they could rent a moving truck, and they were sold out too. Next, they checked the bus schedule, and the bus they needed doesn't come to town every day. They'd have to take a few buses, and it would take two days, not to mention the expense. They'd have to stay in town for one to two days before they could even get a bus.

They went to the hostel and were told it would cost $35 per person per night. They looked around, and it would be sharing a crappy room on bunk beds with several other people. They decided not to stay there because of the time and money involved. They didn't have much money, so they decided to hitchhike. They assumed that they'd have to inch their way to Orange County because it was 260 miles away. They were very grateful that I could take them almost the entire way.

Travis lived in Ecuador and worked remotely as a web developer. Ecuador wasn't very expensive to live in, and he liked it there. Taylor and Nick still lived in Colorado. They were in that stage of reevaluating if they wanted to work in a cubicle for the rest of their life. They were going through a similar situation as Sam—what is their true purpose in life?

I thoroughly enjoyed talking with the guys. They were upbeat and fun. Taylor said, "It's a good thing *you* picked us up because we all smell so bad; we're immune and don't notice it!" He was right. We all stunk badly but stunk equally bad.

The sun disappeared, and we hit traffic once we reached the north side of LA. Thankfully, it cleared up fairly quickly. We made it to my house around 9:00 pm. They came inside to use the bathroom and ordered an Uber. I took their picture in front of my house, and we exchanged contact information. They said, "Because of you, we get to eat lasagna, swim in the pool, and sleep in a bed tonight!" They left, and the Uber cost $35, just like I estimated.

I walked inside my house and said hello to my cat. Then I immediately got into the shower. It had been nine days since I showered. I washed my long hair multiple times and scrubbed my skin over and over.

On the trail, I rinsed my legs and arms a few times in the lakes. I used Wilderness Wipes to wash my face once a day, but that was about it.

As the water rushed over me, I couldn't help but beam with joy. I was overcome with a certain feeling.

My mind replayed the moment I drove away from the hitchhikers and debated whether or not I should turn around. I had so many times like that in my marriage where I wanted to help people; sometimes, it meant turning around. But my husband would talk me out of it, "It's not your problem. You've already passed them. Just keep going." I would listen to him and feel guilty that I should have helped. Maybe it was a stranger, but I knew they needed help.

It hit me like a ton of bricks in that shower. My husband was keeping me from being me—the Christy that God created. Without him, I listened to my gut, and I turned around. Because I had turned around, I had company for the four-hour drive. They brought me joy, talking about our adventures. They were able to get home that night and didn't have to spend a lot of money. It was an experience that I wouldn't have received if I didn't listen to my gut. I didn't need my husband. In fact, I needed to be without him.

I climbed into bed after taking some ibuprofen. I hugged my comforter and pillows. I stretched my legs out because I could and drifted off to sleep.

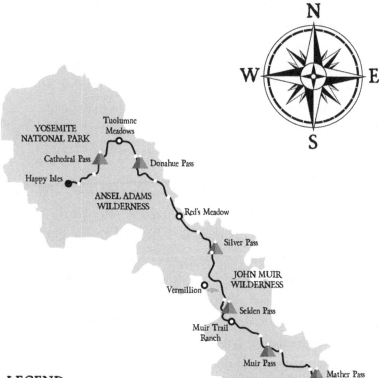

N

W   E

S

YOSEMITE
NATIONAL PARK

Tuolumne
Meadows

Cathedral Pass

Happy Isles

Donahue Pass

ANSEL ADAMS
WILDERNESS

Red's Meadow

Silver Pass

JOHN MUIR
WILDERNESS

Vermillion

Selden Pass

Muir Trail
Ranch

Muir Pass

Mather Pass

Pinchot Pass

KINGS CANYON
NATIONAL PARK

Glen Pass

Mount
Whitney

Whitney
Portal

Forester Pass

SEQUOIA
NATIONAL PARK

LEGEND

Pass	Elevation (feet)
Cathedral	9,703
Donahue	11,073
Silver	10,754
Selden	10,898
Muir	11,975
Mather	12,100
Pinchot	10,050
Glen	11,926
Forester	13,160
Mt. Whitney	14,494

— Dots indicate my campsites

After the JMT

I woke up to a quiet, empty house. I had texted my family at Whitney Portal to let them know I finished and that I'd contact them later. My family lived in St. Louis, Missouri, but my husband was living with his mom 15 minutes away from our house in Lakewood, California.

I didn't turn on the TV or any music. I needed quiet. I read that some people experience depression when they return from a long-distance hike because life is so different outside of the trail.

I was starting to feel the effects—not of depression—but sensory overload. Spending three weeks in the mountains and returning to a place like Los Angeles felt overcrowded and overwhelming. I didn't want noise and distraction.

I opened my fridge, and all I had was an apple. I ate it and didn't feel very hungry. I weighed myself and lost 14 pounds in those three weeks. I looked down at my legs, and they were strong and powerful—I gained muscle. I also noticed that my legs were red, and I had significant tan lines. I thought I developed a good base tan and didn't bother putting sunscreen on the last day. It was hot and sunny and turned my tan red.

My skin was extremely dry and started peeling around my fingertips and feet within days. It's unavoidable in the Sierras. They are dry, and it's rough on your skin.

I started to empty my backpack and washed my sleeping bag. Then I took my tent to the backyard, set it up, and hosed it down. It quickly dried in the sun. It was sad seeing my temporary house in my well-manicured backyard. It didn't belong there; it belonged in the wilderness.

I opened my bear can, and there was still a decent amount of food left. This was because I didn't eat my dinners the night I met Tori or the evening after hiking Whitney. I had included a couple of extra meals and snacks just in case I got stranded.

Looking at my items, there are a few things I was so happy to have brought with me:

- My handkerchief that hung from my front strap. I used it to wipe off the sweat from my face.
- My Thermarest sleeping pad was a pain to blow up and deflate every day, but it was worth it. I usually have a hard time sleeping in a tent because my hips hurt (I'm a side sleeper). The pad (and the foam pad I put underneath) helped me sleep pretty soundly. Or maybe it was pure exhaustion each night.
- My tent and sleeping bag were designed for tall people. It slightly added bulk and weight, but

I'm glad I had items that fit me better than the standard ones.

- My Jetboil was so easy and quick to use—I loved it. It boiled quickly, kept the wind out, and worked as my bowl so I didn't have to bring dishes.
- Ibuprofen was a lifesaver for pain and reducing inflammation.
- D-mannose because it prevents UTI's and I'm very prone to them.
- I brought calcium and magnesium because of my recent removal of two parathyroid glands and I was happy to have both to help with my recovery and sore muscles.
- My trekking poles were my handrails and alleviated pressure from my knees during descents. I don't think I saw a single JMT hiker without them.
- The two packets of hand warmers were perfect on those snowy days.
- My sandals felt so good to wear around camp in the evenings to give my feet a break from my hiking shoes. They were also easy to get on for early morning bathroom needs.
- Shoe inserts really helped because there were so many rocks digging into my feet.
- I'm happy that my toiletries were all scent-free.

There were a few other items that I could have done without or weren't ideal:

- I didn't need so much lotion. I brought a small bottle, but it could have been a very tiny bottle. I usually use a lot of lotion in real life and was worried about dry skin. The thing is, my skin was almost always covered in dust. It was terrible enough rubbing in sunscreen through the dust. Also, the sunscreen acted like a lotion.

- I didn't need some of the extra food, but it's hard to say not to bring it because you might need it. I struggled to have an appetite most days, possibly because of the elevation. I wish I brought more tasty foods and more variety. Mashed potatoes and olive oil were amazing out there!

- I didn't use much soap because I usually just washed my Jetboil with a washcloth and water. Because my dishes were so minimal and it was just me, it didn't seem necessary to do much more.

- I never once used the foldable bucket that I planned to use to wash my dishes and clothes (to keep the soap out of the lakes and rivers). The only times I washed my clothes were at Tuolumne Meadows, Red's Meadow, VVR, and MTR. I used my detergent at Tuolumne Meadows, but the other places all had soap for purchase. I didn't bother trying to wash clothes on the trail after they didn't dry at Tuolumne Meadows. It was too cold out for them to dry in time to wear the next day.

- I preferred my Wild Ideas Bear canister, but at high elevations and the cold, I often had a hard

time turning the coin I brought to open it. I wish
I would have sprayed some WD40 to ensure the
knobs turned more easily.
- I didn't use emergency supplies like the whistle or
compass, but it's still necessary to keep them on
you.

The end-of-season survey results came out and Glen
Pass was voted the most difficult, which I completely
agree with. The other thing that stood out to me were
the top issues people had that year. They involved hiking
partners. It was challenging for people to be in agree-
ment of where to stop for lunch and for the night, and for
how long. In some cases, people fought over it.

There were other cases where someone in the group
had a minor injury, or didn't want to finish the trail. That
led to them trying to decide how to continue on their
own. In the end, I'm happy that I hiked solo.

I didn't have to compromise on when and where to
stop, or for how long. I met lots of people that kept me
company when I needed it.

I never saw a bear during my three weeks out there,
but I saw bear droppings shortly after leaving my campsite at Forester Pass. Based on the survey, bears didn't
seem to be a problem for people.

After spending the day emptying my backpack, I
knew that I needed dinner. I couldn't bring myself to go
to the grocery store, so I went through the drive-through
at El Pollo Loco. As I waited for the girl to get my food,
I couldn't help but notice that her hat had a slogan to get
people to buy more chicken.

I sat there thinking about that hat. There were some people, somewhere, sitting in a boardroom, thinking about clever slogans to put on hats that encourage people to buy *more*. That is what has become of the human race. Lives lived in boardrooms and cubicles. And for what? To get people to buy more, to consume more.

One of the things that made the JMT so special was that everything I needed, I carried on my back. My house, food, water, entertainment, and clothes. All of it fit in a backpack. I didn't have to decide what to wear each day. I knew I was wearing the outfit that I didn't wear the day before.

I wasn't inundated with choice. Even my food choices were between a couple of items. Weeks after the JMT, I flew to Colorado for a wedding, and I walked through the airport. Nonstop signs and booths were begging me to buy something: a tasty dessert or a cute souvenir. We live in a world where we have to say *no* constantly. Those constant decisions exhaust us until we give in and buy something. We eat something we shouldn't. We buy something we shouldn't. Everywhere we look, there is a brightly colored sign, a building, or a road—concrete everywhere.

I had a few days before I had to return to work on Monday. I talked with my family, and it snapped me out of my quiet time. Then I messaged my husband. He congratulated me and said he was proud of what I accomplished. I couldn't help but notice he didn't ask to see me. I asked if he wanted to get breakfast the next day, and he agreed.

He didn't have much time because he had to go to

work. I told him about my time and gave him highlights. I asked if he sent me a letter because I didn't receive one. He said that he did send one, and "it must have been lost in the mail." I doubted him and asked what it said. He gave me a pathetic, generic overview, "You know . . . that I was proud of you and encouraged you, saying you could do this. I knew you could. You always accomplish what you put your mind to."

I wanted to believe him. I didn't want to believe that he forgot about me and then lied to cover it up. But my mind knew—that's why we were separated after all—the lies. My heart refused to believe it.

For a week, I anxiously checked the mail. I even called MTR to see if a letter arrived for me. One day, a postcard arrived from a friend. It was sent to the wrong P.O. Box and eventually made it to MTR and was forwarded to me. That's when I knew that he never sent a letter. His instinct was to lie, like usual.

I went back to work that Monday and received a warm welcome from my coworkers and friends. They couldn't believe how much weight I had lost and how tan I was. They wanted to hear all about it. I told them how I met amazing people, got stuck in a hail storm, hiked Mount Whitney in the snow, and picked up hitchhikers. After all that work getting a permit, I told them that I wasn't asked for it once. I only saw a Park Ranger once or twice, and they didn't ask. Other hikers said they were asked a few times.

People were so intrigued about my adventure, and the H.R. Director (my boss) said that I should host a lunch-and-learn. We held those occasionally, but they were usually company-sponsored and involved some financial or life-planning advice. She said I could use the conference room and tell people to bring their lunch, play a video, and tell them about the experience.

I had made a few videos for the company earlier in the year that were well-received, so I got to work on putting together a video (more like a slideshow) of my experience. I put it on Vimeo (Christy Hikes the John Muir Trail 2016) and sent out invites to my lunch-and-learn.

I brought in some items for show-and-tell, like my sleeping bag, sleeping pad and my bear can. I couldn't believe it when 40 people showed up! I stood at the podium and narrated the video while people asked some questions. I was in my element—talking about something I loved. Seeing the look in their eyes was one of the best things I have experienced.

Our usual company culture was that of work. But that day, in that hour, I was able to bring a little fun into their day. We laughed and got comfortable. I think they were so intrigued because if *I* could do something like that, so could they.

I went to lunch with Barry the day I got back to work since he's the one who told me about the trail. I told him about the highlights and how beautiful the trail was. I also said that my hair had been falling out the past couple of months, and he asked, "Are you eating?" I had lost my appetite on the trail, but it was coming back. I found out later that the hair loss was from the stress of my separation.

A year later, Barry left the company, and we went to our last lunch. He said, "I don't know if I ever told you, but I'm very impressed you hiked the entire JMT. Most people probably think you just went for a long walk, but I know that trail. I've researched it a lot, and it is a no-joke trail. It's intense."

I really appreciated hearing that. That's just it—the JMT is not just 222+ miles; the entire trail is at high elevation. Each day, I climbed up 2,000 to 3,000 feet and another 2,000 to 3,000 down. The trail is almost never flat. Even when it looks flat, it's not. You have to constantly worry about rocks lurking under the dirt, waiting to trip you. There are hundreds of river and stream crossings. The weather changes rapidly and you can't predict it.

But the scenery, peace, and comradery make all of it worth it.

My New Life

When I returned from the JMT, I was separated from my husband and still wasn't sure what to do. I thought about my marriage many times while hiking, but there wasn't a sudden lightbulb moment that made things clear.

Within a couple of weeks, my friend Jenny had a party with her past real estate clients. I talked to my friend Rick, who was a decade older than me. He knew both my husband and I, and met us at the same time. I gave him a summary in five minutes about what was going on and why we were separated.

I asked Rick, "Do you think we can make it work?"

Without hesitation, he said, "No."

I asked him why he thought that. Rick went on to explain, "You are the only one investing in the relationship. He isn't. You can't make him invest, and you can't make a relationship work with one person not investing."

That hit me hard. Rick was right. I had only seen my husband a few times in the last several months, and each time, I initiated seeing him. While he kept telling me that he didn't want our marriage to end and that I was the love of his life, his actions were far from it.

Rick liked my husband, but he knew I wasn't in a healthy relationship. Rick told me how his first marriage didn't work out and how he met his current wife in his late 30s. They were great together, and he reassured me that I didn't need to worry about meeting someone in my 30s.

I decided to start seeing a therapist on my own. In the first session, I explained the situation—all of the lies and how we separated. At the end of the session, the therapist said, "I think you've made up your mind, but you're having a hard time processing it emotionally."

I cried throughout every session. The therapist was right. I knew in my heart that I needed to divorce my husband, but I couldn't accept it emotionally. I still loved him, but I knew he wasn't good for me. I don't think he even wanted to stay married, but he would never pull that trigger.

The therapist got me to see that my husband was a manipulator. While he kept telling me that he was too depressed to take action to save our marriage, like going to therapy or seeing me, he was attending football games and motorcycle shows.

My husband wasn't the only person to blame. My identity had become wrapped up in helping him, whether it was with school, his job, or life in general. I made my life about helping him because it felt good to me to help him. I am responsible for that—he didn't make me to do that.

The therapist also helped me to see that I was crying so much because I was grieving. I was experiencing a loss—the loss of the life I built with my husband for more than a decade. I was losing the future that I thought I was going to have. I was losing the person that I thought was my life partner.

Each week, I told the therapist I was torn on what to do. After two months, she told me, "You found your strength on the JMT, and the longer you stay with him, the more you're losing that strength."

By that November, I asked my husband to come over. We talked for a couple of hours, and he thought it was just a regular talk about our relationship, until I said, "I think we should get divorced."

My husband stood up, upset, at the idea. I was surprised and asked him, "What did you think was going to happen? You've barely seen me in six months. You've done absolutely nothing to prevent a divorce."

He explained, "I am always thinking about you. I think about things to say, but then I get afraid that it will push you further away. So I don't say anything."

I said, "Well, you just guaranteed a way to push me away. I'm tired of trying to get you to act, to say something, to go to therapy."

I filed for divorce in December, and he signed the papers on Christmas Eve. In California, the divorce isn't legal until six months after both parties sign. I had to keep him on my health and life insurance. Those six months dragged the pain out.

I spent months crying, even at work. I used to rarely cry, but the divorce broke me. I was worried that my husband wouldn't be okay. I was worried that I'd never find the right life partner.

I couldn't get myself to say the word "divorce" because the pain would choke my throat.

Then in May, a month before our divorce was final, I found out that he was dating someone who lived a mile from my house. He lied about it, of course, until I told him that I knew about her. He was happy and giddy—he would be just fine without me, even though for so long he told me he wouldn't be.

Once he moved his stuff out of the house that day in May, he drove away in his U-Haul after kissing my cheek, and I haven't heard from him since.

A year later, I was at the grocery store and ran into my ex-husband and his girlfriend. He walked away from her while she checked out the cheeses. He also walked away from me, pretending he didn't know me. Twelve years together, and we turned into people who didn't even acknowledge each other.

Once the divorce was final, I changed my last name back to my maiden name. That's when coworkers realized that I had gotten divorced. It got easier and easier to say the word divorce. Slowly everyone knew, and just like that, I was single again.

My ex-husband used the money I had to pay him out with to take his new girlfriend on trips and cruises. A year later, he proposed to her, and they got married a year after that. They recently had a son.

Certain things were clear to me after hiking the JMT—I wanted more adventures. When I returned to work, it felt like I hadn't even been gone. Everything was the same, but I was different. I couldn't help but think about that feeling—how everything that I needed was on my back.

Back in the real world, I worked hard at a job for good money, but what was it getting me? Sure, I could pay for my house and life, but it was lonely. I would often lay on my couch in the evenings, realizing just how quiet my place was. I worked so hard to attain that house and be promoted at work, but was it worth it?

I was living for work, only getting three weeks of vacation time a year. Most of my friends were married and/or had kids. I didn't have family nearby. It was just me and the house. It was an empty feeling. I was working for material items. I didn't grow up with much money and now that I had it, it lost its luster.

A year after hiking the JMT, I used my three weeks of vacation time to go to Scandinavia. I started in Norway on a nine-day hiking and kayaking tour through the fjords with eight other people and two guides. It was stunning, and I had the time of my life.

Once the tour ended, I traveled by myself to Oslo, Denmark, and Sweden. I hadn't gone on such a long and distant trip alone in a very long time. I was nervous at first—I don't even speak the languages.

I ended up loving the ten days traveling by myself. I visited the places that I wanted, met people on tours and around town, and ate when I wanted.

When I returned to Los Angeles, I sat in the Uber, realizing that I didn't want to be back. I didn't feel relieved that I was "home." For the first time in 15 years, I didn't want to be in L.A.

Within the next couple of months, my neighbor sold

their house, which was almost identical to mine, and got a ton of money. Then, a realtor knocked on my door, asking if I wanted to sell my house because they needed inventory. I started doing the math and realized that I could get enough money from my house to travel for two or two and a half years full-time.

I prayed, and God showed me that it was time for me to leave and to trust Him with the plans He has for me.

I spent six months quietly planning my departure, doing some repairs on the house, and hosting family members from out of state.

Then in June 2018, two years after hiking the JMT, I quit my job of 11 years, sold my house, and put my stuff in storage. I hit the road with the Alaska Highway in my sights.

I spent time in Oregon and Washington and even got to backpack in Olympic National Park for a few days with some friends. Then I drove to Canada and eventually on the Alaska Highway, all the way to Fairbanks.

After four months, I returned to L.A. to visit and was quickly back in Whistler, Canada, where I spent a month. After that, I flew to Thailand for a month, Vietnam for a month, and Australia for six months. I drove around the entire country of Australia, having a blast exploring the beaches and the outback.

I returned to the U.S. and spent time in my hometown, St. Charles, Missouri. I bought a house there while I was in Australia and spent a few months moving my stuff from L.A. to set the house up on Airbnb.

I flew to Switzerland with plans to see Eastern Europe, and after ten days, the Covid-19 travel bans started. I had to return home. After a couple of months, I road-tripped around National Parks in Montana, Wyoming, Colorado, and Utah.

Like many people, Covid disrupted my life and travel plans. After the road trip, I went back to Missouri and stayed with my parents while setting up another Airbnb and finishing this book.

I'm still single and haven't dated anyone. I had no interest in dating the first year of my divorce. Since then, there have been men that I liked, but it never turned into anything. I don't want to get stuck in another relationship where I'm the one putting in all of the effort. I want an equal partner who I can trust.

It's been five years since I hiked the JMT. At times, it feels like it was just yesterday that I was laughing with my trail friends and climbing up those mountains. Sometimes when I hike trails with a similar look or a smell to the JMT, I'm instantly transported to those days. I see my dusty legs and shoes, and I think about the dirt that accompanied me for those three weeks.

Other times, it feels like a lifetime ago. It was the start of the rumblings in my soul—the start of knowing my life was about to change. It was the beginning of knowing that God wanted me to break free from that life. He wanted me to be the person He created me to be. I felt it deep within me. I knew my life would look very different; I just had no idea *how* it would look.

Since hiking the JMT, I have hiked in Norway, Olympic National Park, Thailand, and Australia. I love hiking, and now I feel like I can handle any trail that comes my way. Whenever a trail becomes difficult, I remind myself that I hiked the JMT solo, and no trail will defeat me.

When I first got the permit to hike the JMT, I had never backpacked before. I'm not someone to go out and do something that extreme without preparing. As one friend once told me, "You take risks in life, but they're calculated risks."

I'm happy that I spent time reading, researching, watching documentaries, and asking people for advice. I was able to complete the JMT in three weeks, solo, because of the preparation and advice.

As I reflect on my journey of the JMT, I feel that things worked out perfectly. I didn't have to deal with any rain until the final night. It was mostly fantastic weather with bright blue skies. I didn't even need bug spray. Every person that I met was meant to be in my path and came at the perfect time.

The JMT is just as much a mental struggle as a physical struggle. Meeting people helps combat those mental challenges. Nobody ever gave me a trail name and I don't think I found out anybody else's trail name, if they were given one. Instead, when I think about the people I met, I think about how they made me *feel*. I think about how they helped me and the conversations we had.

While I didn't come home with *all* the answers, I gained my strength on that trail. For that, I'll always be grateful.

Where Are They Now?

I've stayed in touch with many people that I met on the JMT through social media and email. I love seeing their lives outside of the trail, what adventures they continue to have, and they are always a reminder to me of the time I spent on the John Muir Trail.

I reached out to some of the people I met and asked them what the JMT meant to them. It's been five years, so I also wanted to see what they've been up to since. Here are summaries of when I saw them last and their responses.

Justin

I found Justin on social media when I was at Red's Meadow and we connected. The business card that he gave me was helpful!

After his backpacking trip in Yosemite, he did one more short backpacking trip, then headed to Utah. He backpacked and visited National Parks; he even met up with a friend in Moab. His final stop was spending a few days in Yellowstone National Park in Wyoming.

Justin told me that moving his bear canister to the inside of his backpack didn't help at all. He said, "Maybe the bear canisters are a big conspiracy!" We agreed that the canister is probably better than trying to hang a bag of food from a tree branch, but they are hard to carry around.

Two years after the JMT, I was in Portland and met up with Justin. He took me on a walk around the city and to the rose garden. Then we grabbed a bite to eat that day and one other day. He had just moved in with his girlfriend. It was great getting to know him better and reconnect about our shared interest in the outdoors and adventures. He continues to backpack, camp, and travel.

Tom

"First off, I was not able to complete the trail. Regrettably, I hurt my knee around day 15 and powered through for a couple more days, traveling slowly, and then spent an entire day just hanging out, burning through food, trying to decide what to do. I was at a section where I worried I was probably going to run out of food because of the slowed progress. I was also worried about getting into a bad spot where I could no longer remove myself from the situation if I kept pushing my injury. It took some doing, but I managed to hobble my way out and lived to fight another day. :)

"I recall being bummed, but I was never so invested that I was willing to ruin my body for it. It was a part of the trip that I hadn't planned for, so it came with its own set of challenges and ensuing adventures which is all I was ever really after. When I got to the trail, it was following a whole host of tumultuous life circumstances. They weren't the reason I went, but they just sort of unfolded around the same time, and I kept telling myself, *well, I have all of my trip booked and permits in place, so . . . I'm going.*

"Looking back, I remember it fondly. I didn't have a lot of expectations going in. By the time I was making my way there, it seemed the perfect culmination to the end of an old chapter of life and the beginning of a new one. It didn't single-handedly and radically change my life or perspective on life, but it helped cement the path that was leading to the future life I was hoping to live.

"Currently, I am married to my amazing wife, Kristin. We live in Colorado, have two badass cats, work at a CBD company and continue to travel when we can. Got them bills, you know!—but working on figuring out that digital nomad thing. :) We travel around the US as much as we can, and as far as our most recent international travels, we spent time in India and then Iceland, and they were both radical."

Paige

"Growing up in San Diego, my first real mountain experience was visiting Yosemite. I never had any interest in the mountains until going to the valley, mind blown by the beauty and serenity of the granite walls and beautiful falls. Being a beach bum and knowing nothing about camping, let alone backpacking, I knew I needed more. I remember setting off to do the Nevada Falls trail and seeing 'John Muir Trail 211 miles.' As I graduated college and all my friends set off for Europe, I set off for the JMT, not knowing what to expect other than where to pick up my food resupplies.

"Going onto the trail with no expectations, the mountains gave me exactly what I needed. Every moment was perfect—from the feelings of total awe to the feelings of total exhaustion, hunger and fear. The best part was sharing these experiences with complete strangers from all over the world, each with their own story. The whole experience filled a void I didn't even know I had.

"After the JMT, I went on to nursing school. I continued to travel any chance I could, seeking out new places to explore with the best co-pilot, Indra (my husky pup), and of course, meeting the most amazing people along the way. I completed nursing school and became an ER nurse working in Inglewood, California, just in time for COVID-19 to strike America. After a very rough year working the frontlines, I am now travel-nursing with my partner in crime, chasing the seasons for the best surf, snow, rock climbs, and more backpacking adventures. My job has been so hard and draining, but these experiences and memories keep me going."

Corey

I connected with Corey and Brianna on social media and loved seeing Corey's glassblowing work and their life in Michigan. A year and a half after the JMT, Corey was briefly in Los Angeles on a trip with his new girlfriend. I asked him what happened to him and Brianna because they had been together for eight years. He said they were drifting apart, and the JMT made it clear that they shouldn't be together. They had hoped it would be a trip to bring them closer together, but they fought a lot on that trip, which I hadn't been aware of.

When they were going to leave the trail at VVR but changed their mind, Corey said it was because of the fighting. Brianna was upset they were hiking with so many people because she wanted the experience to be just them. Corey is really social and loves meeting new people. He pointed out to her that when they spent time with people, she enjoyed it. She agreed and decided to stay. In the end, it was clear that they wanted different things.

Corey had met someone else, and I agreed to meet him and his new girlfriend for dinner.

As soon as I saw Corey, I was elated! It had been a year and a half, and I was instantly brought back to our time in the wilderness. His girlfriend, Geri, was super sweet, and I liked her right away. She was more than a foot shorter than Corey, but they were perfect for each other. I still liked Brianna, but I could tell that Geri complimented Corey's outgoing personality. I told them a story of things going on in my life, and they listened with such enthusiasm that I felt valued. I was touched that they made time to see me on their trip.

A couple of years later, they got engaged! It's been five years since the JMT, and they are set to be married in Yosemite!

"The JMT was the most thrilling experience of my life so far. The scenery was on a scale I'd never seen before. The challenges it made me overcome as an inexperienced backpacker was very valuable to know I am capable of big things if I just do it.

"The people I met and saw along the way were very inspiring, particularly the different ages. The elderly people showed me that it's never too late to adventure and you're never too old to try and stay active. The younger people I saw gave me a good perspective into taking the time while you can to travel and not be a slave to the grind.

"It's been several years now and it's already sinking in how quickly life slips by if you let it. The JMT most of all taught me to get out there and experience the world while you have the opportunity. Since hiking the JMT I definitely find that I'm seeking out a different type of camping recreation than what I knew from my childhood. I know it's made a lifelong impression on finding adventures in nature vs tourist hot spots and gimmicky attractions. I respect the areas more that are kept pure from our human influence and have a lot more passion for being an advocate of the outdoors. I'm so thankful for that experience and I still can't believe it happened sometimes.

"Recently my fiancé Geri and I went and visited Yosemite and hiked portions of the JMT—it was so surreal!! We actually decided to plan our elopement and have a mini-mony at Glacier Point. So you can say Yosemite had its impact on me lol. Geri felt the same way and actually teared up leaving the valley, I knew we made the right choice. Next month Yosemite will hold an even greater place in our hearts when we officially tie the knot amongst that incredible backdrop of Mother

Nature's beauty. Someday hopefully soon, Geri and I will hike the JMT together and I can't wait!"

Bolivar

Bolivar finished at Whitney portal the day before me. When he arrived at the bottom, he discovered that his mom was waiting there! She wanted to surprise him and thankfully, Bolivar was on track to meet the itinerary he sent his family.

About a week after he returned, he went to the movie theater, where he enjoyed a large popcorn, soda, and air conditioning!

"I have bittersweet memories of the JMT. It was a beautiful, amazing experience and, in many ways, the ultimate physical and emotional challenge of my life. It also marks the beginning of the end of my marriage. I was so excited to see my wife and kids when I got home, but rather than receive the warm welcome from my wife; she stopped talking to me for several weeks. Things only got progressively worse after that until she asked me for a divorce.

"A couple of years later, I returned to the top of Whitney with my two boys after hiking the High Sierra Trail from Sequoia National Park. It was wonderful to find myself on the last stretch of the JMT again and, this time to be sharing it with my kids.

"The people I met on the trail and the camaraderie was one of the unexpected highlights of my hike on the JMT. Walking alone through the forests and meadows, up and down the rocky passes, was peaceful and meditative. It was something that I needed, but coming across fellow hikers and engaging with others who had a similar love of nature and a desire to challenge themselves was inspiring, filled my cup, and was a welcome break from the relentless isolation and, at times, desolation.

"I'm still in touch, albeit infrequently, with a handful of folks I met on the trail, and thinking about it now, with all that has changed in my life since I hiked the JMT, I still feel a bond with them, and perhaps it's time to reconnect a little and share some photos, stories, and memories."

Thomas, Chresten, Jerry, and Tom

Thomas and I exchanged emails a month after completing the JMT, and he explained that their mule drop that was supposed to be delivered to Kearsarge Lake was delivered to Charlotte Lake (and a day earlier than planned). Tom and Chresten decided to bail after hiking over Kearsarge Pass into Independence. Chresten's feet were extremely blistered, and she was in a lot of pain. Tom was trail weary and wanted to return to Washington for a travel-trailer adventure with his wife.

Thomas and Jerry thought about bailing, but after Chresten, Jerry, and Thomas called the mule supply company, they agreed to meet them if Thomas and Jerry hiked over Kearsarge Pass. Thomas said, "Bastards made us hike two miles and 2,000 feet of vertical and refused to meet us at the agreed-upon meeting place of Kearsarge Lake. Then they not only cashed Jerry's check, but also charged his credit card making double the $525.00. Jerry was able to dispute this charge, but we also lost our deposit with the shuttle in Lone Pine we had reserved for Sept 25th."

Thomas and Jerry continued the JMT but experienced a rain deluge with wind gusts over 60 MPH. They stayed the night a mile below Forester Pass at an unnamed lake on a granite slab (likely the same spot I camped). Jerry only had a 25° bag, and there was only one partially wind-protected site, so they joined forces in Jerry's tent to stay warm.

When Thomas and Jerry summited Mount Whitney, it didn't go as planned. Thomas was feeling spry and flew up the last two miles to the summit, arriving half an hour before Jerry. Thomas said, "It's amazing how fast you can travel when you shed 45 pounds." Unfortunately, Jerry was experiencing nausea, light-headedness, and vertigo as he got near the avalanche chutes. They got him to a lower elevation right away, and he was okay.

Thomas described their exit from Trail Camp, "The exit from Trail Camp was both beautiful and satisfying to complete the trail. I had a bacon cheeseburger, the first in a couple of years, as I generally eschew beef. The beer was a real treat to enjoy after so many days without a cold one. On the way down the Whitney Portal trail, we met Makayla, a hiker from the Midwest. We chatted about the beer and chocolate ice cream awaiting our return to civilization. Her dad graciously gave us a ride to Lone Pine as Makayla was waiting for her group to exit. The next morning Jerry & I boarded a bus to drop us at Carson City, where a buddy from Incline Village picked us up with some homemade cookies and beverages."

Thomas and Jerry finished the JMT five days after I did. Within a few weeks, Thomas went on an eight-day Idaho/Washington fishing trip with some buddies. He told me, "The one thing I would have preferred to do more of on the JMT is fishing. When our resupply at Kearsarge Lakes went awry and delayed our exit by one day, a stringer of brook trout made up for the lack of dehydrated food and was a most welcome change to freshness."

Chresten

"Growing up and still living at Lake Tahoe, I've back-packed my whole life. Until I joined some friends to backpack the JMT, I hadn't done any long-distance trails. I really enjoyed the trek, the scenery, the people I met along the way (but Christy was the most fun!), and the overall physical challenge of such an undertaking.

"I'm totally hooked and am looking forward to doing more (retirement is just a handful of years away!). Being out on the trail, the one thing I missed the most was my favorite trail companion, my Siberian Husky, Mica. There are parts of the trail she is allowed on, so I've been back to one of those areas a couple of times with her. Island Pass and Thousand Island Lake are stunningly beautiful, and it was fun to spend a few days just exploring the area with my best furry friend.

"My backpacking buddies and I continue to ski, hike, and backpack together, including an epic climb of Mt. Kilimanjaro in Tanzania. My first, and chances are only, of the world's 7 Summits!"

Jerry

"Completing the JMT as my first ever backpacking trip, at age 69, from Tuolumne Meadows to Whitney Portal (235 miles in 23 days) with three other friends was so filled with pleasures, and problems, that it has deeply influenced my life. The pleasures I encountered in that trek now lead me out the door nearly every day (and some overnights) into the mountains surrounding my home in Nevada near the north shore of Lake Tahoe. 'Follow the water, find the vista, revel in the meadow' are my mantras as I hike with my camera seeking out fauna and flora. Sitting on a crest looking through my lens down onto raptors soaring below is a reminder of all the wonders of the JMT.

"Problems (summarized in my trail name 'Pig Pen') were not absent. As a rookie backpacker, I learned a number of life lessons that apply to preserving my body into its advanced stages of life. Not properly eating dehydrated food, nor cleaning my body in the frigid waters of the JMT, led to infections and surgeries upon my return to 'civilization.' I now see the natural world as a place to cleanse myself, both mentally and physically. Those lessons had not appeared in my previous 3 week adventure, sailing solo from American Samoa to Honolulu at age 43, in the comforts of a 42 foot sailboat. Thank you, JMT."

Trevor

"I can still hear the gravel crunch under my trail shoes as I take each step—moving at a consistent pace to chase down the miles that lead to the next campsite. I bathe in the forest breeze, look out at the expansive view and feel the weight of that darn pack. To say the JMT made an impact is an understatement. I still often reference moments of that trail when I want to ground myself and go to a happy place.

"The JMT was my first big adventure for 'myself.' Not a journey for career advancement or family vacation. It was something I chose to do for me. That was BIG, as I tend to do what others want. It wasn't at all easy. It will run you through all the emotions of an Adventure Movie. But when you come out the other side, man, is it worth it!

"This JMT adventure gave me strength and led to countless new life experiences. I travelled to Costa Rica on my own, learning to surf; I built up enough endurance to complete Mountain Trail runs up to 25km; I Motorcycled through the Western US; I completed an Olympic Distance Triathlon.

"The JMT was a life experience that I'm grateful for—one that I hope to share with my kids when we want a break from technology and reconnect with nature. The impact was definitely mind-opening, and I wanted to hold onto that energy. I ended up getting a tree tattooed on my calf to remind me to always choose the path of adventure. I will go back someday!"

Sam

"At the time I started the JMT, I was seeking big adventures and major life changes. Through walking, I was reminded of the simplicity of life on the trail. I connected with many other walkers. I saw beauty in each day. I felt alive again. This solo adventure was more than I could've asked for. I felt independent, confident, joyful, and grateful on the trail. The JMT is one of the most beautiful places I've been, and I know I'll be back again.

"After the JMT, I wasn't ready for the adventure to be over. When I finished walking, I explored California for a while longer before deciding to move to the Bay Area. I knew no one and didn't have a job there, but that was part of the adventure. I stayed in the Bay Area for about a year before traveling to India to become a yoga teacher. Eventually, I headed back to the East Coast, where my roots are.

"Currently, I spend lots of time outdoors seeking adventures, new places, and views as often as possible. Usually, I hike locally in New England, where I work as a teacher. Somehow I've found my way back to similar crossroads I was at when I started the JMT. I'm considering a big move and a career change in the very near future. New adventures are on the horizon, and I can't wait."

Nick

"The JMT came at a point where I was at a crossroads with what I was going to do with the rest of my life. Prior to the JMT, I spent eight months in Uganda, and I had to decide whether it would become a continual part of who I am. Unexpectedly, the JMT turned into somewhat of a soul-searching experience. Three weeks in the wilderness to think, pray, and discuss ideas was what I needed.

"The JMT experience didn't exactly match my romanticized idea of a soul-searching adventure where there is nothing but gentle grades and breathtaking views. There was a lot of misery and pain involved, and the majority of the time is spent looking down at the trail in front of you. It was the monotonous time between the grand peaks and great views that was the most important for me.

"With all the time that the JMT gave me to reflect on life, I ended up making the decision to go back to Uganda, where I have now lived for the last four years. I have been working with a Christian non-profit ministry that works with vulnerable children and families in slum communities. Last month, I married a wonderful Ugandan woman named Jocelyn.

"I look forward to taking her to visit the U.S. someday and sharing with her my love for the Colorado outdoors."

Tori

"Meeting Christy was a lesson in surviving without Google Maps! After posting a message to a trailhead sign, asking every hiker we saw pass after dark, to seeing her flashlight come down the trail, it was pure fun to meet up with her on her journey. It was definitely an 'I can't believe it really worked!' moment.

"We were bringing her snacks on the trail, but I think we ate half of what we brought her as we stayed up late under the stars! While my experience was just one day on Christy's adventure, my feet hurt for days to come. I was inspired by her strength and no-problem-too-big attitude, and I hope one day to spend some time on a long through-hike myself.

"Since hiking to meet Christy, I have continued to

explore and enjoy the great outdoors! My favorite back-packing trip recently was in Glacier National Park, and I have been to 14 National Parks in the last 12 months. To me, the most important part of the outdoors is seeing people in a common element stripped down of titles or circumstance with everyone just trying to put one foot in front of the next in hopes Mother Nature rewards us with her beauty or her wisdom!"

12
24

Made in the USA
Las Vegas, NV
31 August 2021